Let's Build ExtraOrdinary Youth Together

Kim C. Metcalfe, Ph.D.

Abbey's Press
Astoria, Oregon

Abbey's Press
Astoria, Oregon
https://xtraordinaryyouth.com/

ISBN: 9781080953882
Printed in the United States of America
Second edition

DEDICATION

Abbey Metcalfe: She is my "why"

This book is written to honor the life of my precious daughter, Abigail Elise Metcalfe, who tragically left this earth shortly after her twenty-first birthday. To honor Abbey's life, I lovingly dedicate my work to the youth of the world. May your caregivers give you the opportunities to build the positive self-image you need to live the extraOrdinary life you deserve!

Dearest Abbey, I love you! You have been my inspiration for building Dr. Kim's ExtraOrdinary Youth and for establishing Abbey's Purple Winged Angels Foundation. I thank you for teaching me the depth of a mother's love and the power that comes with it when we allow love to flow freely.

I envision a world where all youth can live productive, meaningful, joyful lives and to create a better future for all of us. My mission is to provide strategies for youth and adults to

ExtraOrdinary Youth

discover who they were born to be and what they were born to do, to be true to themselves and to fulfill their purpose as significant members of society.

Preface

How Much Difference Can One Adult REALLY Make?

Today's young people are more distracted than any generation in history. Between social media, TV, YouTube, music, movies, advertisements and the relentless pressure to fit in with their peers, modern youth are like tiny corks bobbing in an ocean of white noise. To make a *lasting* difference, we must become the clearest, loudest and most profound "voices" in their lives.

My name is Dr. Kim Metcalfe. In 2012, I lost my only biological daughter, Abbey, to suicide. Abbey was not a "troubled teen" by most people's definition. I loved her, nurtured her, raised her with spiritual guidance and made sure she had everything I didn't have growing up. There was nothing, or so I thought, that placed her in the category of "at risk youth," which is defined as *a child who is less likely to transition successfully into adulthood.*

On the day of her suicide, Abbey spent time doing ordinary things as we made plans for her upcoming wedding. As a practicing developmental scientist and psychologist, I was shocked to get the 3a.m. call that she was in the hospital struggling for what would be her last few breaths.

Since that horrid night, I've learned that almost fifty percent of young people in the U.S. are exposed to the *same risk factors* that drove Abbey to suicide. I call them the "invisible children" of our society. The question is, how do you know who these children are, and how much of a difference can you really make? This book will equip you to:

1. Identify the invisible children in your life.
2. Build meaningful connections with them.
3. Help them develop into whole young adults.
4. Empower them to discover their authentic purpose.

Read this book. Use it. Wear it out. It will equip you to become such a force of influence in young people's lives that you won't have to wait on the "right" politicians to be elected or the "right" policies to give your kids the kind of world you want them to inherit.

ACKNOWLEDGMENTS

I want to acknowledge my editor Seth Czerepak, who truthfully is so much more than a brilliant editor. Seth is a personal development specialist and author. He used his experience and background to add clarity and depth to this book. Seth brought to this work his profound understanding of the "reader,"—what the reader really wants and needs. He is sensitive about the reader's time and remains focused on not wasting it. Thank you, Seth I am more grateful than words can express, you are in a word, remarkable!

A special thank you to my friend and colleague Penny G. Davis MS, who lovingly contributed to this work and authored the bonus chapter (14) *Insecure vs Secure Attachments*. She has extensive knowledge on the impact that insecure attachment has on young people and shares some beneficial strategies incorporated in Part B of the *Positive Youth Guidance System*.

I want to acknowledge my dear, late husband, Professor Alfred L. Parker whose love, tenderness, and devotion surely pulled me through the darkest days of my life. Thank you, my love, you are not forgotten.

Thank you to my heart children, Abbey (my Iranian daughter who chose Abigail for her American name), Amanda, Annabel, Demi, Nancy, Majid, and Sarah. You were rays of light in the darkness. You always showed up when I needed you, and you always, always made me feel loved and special.

To my mother, who provided meaningful connections with me until the day she drew her last breath. She planted the seeds that allowed me to face every challenge—even my greatest tragedy—with love. Thank you, mommy, I miss you!

To Emily and Mandi, I realize that losing your sister is a great tragedy for each of you—I was not the only one enduring great pain. Thank you for all the learning experiences you give me—each one offers me the opportunity to stretch and to grow. You are both my reasons for staying, for pushing forward, for choosing life, for choosing purpose, for choosing to try to change things for others.

I want to acknowledge Keely Worthy and Elizabeth Padilla—Abbey's best friends who continue to be a loving part of my life. Thank you both for loving Abbey and for keeping her alive with your memories of her—for never letting her go, and for never letting me go! I find peace and comfort in your love for Abbey and me!

Finally, I want to acknowledge my current partner Stephen, who kept me moving, held me, and encouraged me when the going got tough. Although my work fills me with meaning, purpose, and joy, I often think of Abbey. It breaks my heart that I discovered these things because of her death instead of before it. Thank you, Stephen, for all the times you held me as I wept. Your love helps me stay grounded in hope and appreciation.

WHY THIS BOOK WORKS

This book works because it focuses on meeting the needs of the whole child (intellectual, creative, social, emotional, and physical), while interacting in ways that promote positive self-image, self-regulation, self-control, and self-confidence. The model is based on sound and consistent research that includes the best parenting, communication, and discipline style for all aged children.

PRESCRIPTION

POSITIVE SELF-IMAGE

"A positive self-image is maintained by those who have the qualities and skills that give them the freedom to choose the lives they live."

- Positive self-esteem
- Self-regulation skills

- Self-control

- Intellectual, creative, emotional, social, and physical skills developed to their full potential

- Identity based on virtues that are used to decide and guide behaviors: Who am I?

- Purpose for a meaningful life (tied to interests and natural talents): What is my purpose?

- Significance: Am I a valuable member of society? What do I contribute?

Everything in this book is designed to inform the reader of why this prescription is appropriate for building young people who get to live the lives of their choosing. Readers will discover why these qualities and skills are necessary, and strategies that deliver the experiences, opportunities and encouragement to fulfill the prescription.

TERMS COMMONLY USED IN THIS BOOK

Meaningful connections. At the heart of a meaningful connection is the adult's desire to:

- Understand, respect, and be sensitive to a young person's developmental, intellectual, creative, emotional, social, physical abilities, needs, and yes, their behaviors.

- Encourage further positive development of the *whole person*.

- Elicit the young person's thinking, ideas, possible solutions to problems, and thinking outside of the box, etc.

- Deliver powerful messages to young people about what we think of them.

- Tell kids that we are on their side, that we love and care about them unconditionally and that we are there to support them despite their mistakes.

Meaningful connections are the most powerful way to say to a young person, "You matter, you are important, you are worthy of my time and patience!" These are the messages which support a positive self-image.

Self-awareness. Conscious knowledge of one's own character, feelings, motives, and desires.

Self-confidence. A feeling of trust in one's abilities, qualities, and judgment.

Self-control. The ability to control oneself, in particular one's emotions and desires or the expression of them in one's behavior, especially in difficult situations.

Self-efficacy. An individual's belief in his or her capacity to execute behaviors necessary to produce specific performance attainments.

Self-esteem. Confidence in one's own worth or abilities; self-respect, based on one's evaluation of abilities, appearance, and personality.

Self-image. The idea one has of one's abilities, appearance, and personality.

Self-regulation. Regulating one's thoughts, considering outcomes of behavior before one acts. This is done prior to using self-control.

The whole child or whole person. Includes the five selves, 1) the cognitive, 2) creative, 3) emotional, 4) social, and 5) physical aspects of each human being.

- **The five selves**—reflected in the whole person.

- **The cognitive self**—the part of the person that thinks, reasons, decides, hypothesizes, analyzes, and synthesizes information.

- **The creative self**—the part of the person that makes something novel and useful to the self or others, out of already existing materials or knowledge (thinking outside the box).

- **The emotional self**—the part of the person that feels and emotes.

- **The social self**—the part of the person who interacts with others.

- **The physical self** — the part of the self that navigates the physical structure through the environment and cares for one's biological physical needs.

When we provide opportunities and experiences that develop the skills and respond appropriately to the needs associated with each of the five selves, we fill the prescription that moves youth into productive, meaningful, joyful, ethical lives—lives lived with integrity (living a life consistent with one's values).

Introduction

This book is a call to action!

If you are a parent and you believe that all a kid needs is love, you are wrong. They need much more. I know this because the catalyst for this book was a great tragedy. A tragedy that may have been prevented if I'd known then what I know now. I'm Dr. Kim C. Metcalfe. I'm a mother who lost her daughter to suicide.

Since Abbey's death in 2012, three friends of mine have also lost their children to suicide. Friends often tell me that they have a friend whose teen or young adult committed suicide. The suicides of Robin Williams, Anthony Bourdain, and Kate Spade remind us that wealth, fame, and good looks don't guarantee a joyful life.

How could these people, who seem to have it together, suddenly turn on themselves and take their own lives? We assume they must have lived tumultuous personal lives—lives riddled with insecurities and the torment of inner demons. But you'd be shocked to discover how many "ordinary" people are at risk for suicide. I'm talking about people you would never suspect as being suicidal or even depressed; people whose friends, coworkers and family members would describe them as "normal," "happy" or even "successful."

Abbey, my only biological child, was raised with her adopted sister who is two years older than her. When Abbey was in 9th grade, long after her father and I had divorced, I remarried. Abbey's stepfather and I adopted a daughter, giving Abbey two sisters, both two years older than her. Until Abbey was in sixth grade, she and her sister were court ordered to move from my home to their father's home, in a neighboring town. Her father was a firefighter whose schedule changed every week, so the moves were inconsistent and very stressful. I knew this was difficult on my children. But, the court wanted to be fair to both parents, a decision which often comes at the expense of the children.

Unfortunately, this cost is usually masked by the belief that kids are resilient, that they'll "bounce right back." It's easy to forget that resilience is a trait of people who have something stable to "bounce back" to—some established sense of who they are and what they're worth. But assuming the former, I watched Abbey survive—even appear to thrive—and was shocked to learn that she took her own life.

I am an educated woman and an expert in the field of developmental psychology. I nurtured, loved, and emotionally supported Abbey. I raised her with spiritual guidance. I made sure she and her sister had everything I didn't have growing up. Birthday parties were made special, with presents, cakes, friends, and games. I was the "room mom" in my children's classrooms. I volunteered when the school asked for volunteers. I served as a field trip chaperone. I attended every back to school night, teacher-parent conference, and every event my children participated in. Abbey and her sister went to school dances and proms, played on a community basketball team, celebrated traditional holidays with family, enjoyed slumber parties, shopping, and movies with male and female friends. Abbey was a brilliant jazz, modern, and hip-hop dancer, who was often selected for solo dance performances. Both Abbey and her sister had all the "stuff" kids want to "fit in," a cell phone, a fast computer and internet, designer clothing, fashionable shoes, plenty of private space in our home to have fun and visit with friends. We lived in an upscale neighborhood. When Abbey learned to drive she was given a car. Why would my daughter, who had all these things and more, choose to end her life? There was nothing, or so I thought, that placed her in the category of "at-risk- youth," which is defined as a child who is less likely to transition successfully into adulthood. This is what I mean when I say that plenty of "normal" people are at risk for suicide.

Before Abbey's death, and long after it, I didn't understand how kids who seemingly have it all, could still be "at-risk" because of an adverse childhood experience. I was shocked when I reviewed the statistics of how many young people have experienced trauma during their childhood, and the various reasons behind the trauma. But no matter what the reasons were, I found that there is a common thread in at-risk-children, and that it's linked to childhood trauma. The common thread has to do with how early life trauma impacts the development of a young person's self-image. The trauma damages something deep inside them. It damages their sense of self-worth, which is a primary contributor to their self-image. Too often, they never recover and develop a healthy self-image.

People with a healthy self-image believe that they're important. They believe that they matter, and that they're valuable, and significant. They believe that they're unconditionally loved and celebrated. But people with a negative self-image doubt their own worth because they haven't received positive messages about themselves. Other times, the messages coming from their family, legal guardians, teachers, school staff, administrators, coaches, mentors, tutors, peers, media, or cultural idols, are inconsistent and confusing. And that is the core of the problem.

The adults in a young person's life serve as "midwives" for the young person's self-image. These adults help the young person develop and bring forth a self-image that will determine how they manage all the adversity and opportunity they'll encounter. This happens by means of the young person's connections (or lack thereof) with the adults in their life. This is a double-edged sword. When the connections are healthy, the result is a child or young adult with an empowering and authentic self-image. But when the connections are unhealthy, or non-existent, the self-image doesn't develop properly. This can be a ticking time bomb as the child becomes an adult.

If I could change just one thing in the lives of abused or traumatized young people, I would increase the number of adults who interact with them in meaningful ways. I would choose to see adults making connections which support the young person's creative, social, and emotional needs. I'd want to see adults paying attention to young people without distractions. I'd want to see them taking the time to hear what matters to the young person, instead of only listening for what matters to the adult.

I'd want adults to support the talents and interests of young people, rather than pushing them toward what the adult wants them to be interested in. I'd want to see adults taking the time to help young people identify their own feelings and the needs attached to those feelings. I'd want to see them providing support for young people and guiding them toward getting their needs met in appropriate ways.

But these connections take time and focus to develop. Sometimes it takes special training, because young people aren't born with training manuals and our culture doesn't require the adults who work with them to undergo developmental education. Nevertheless, when adults are too busy to provide support for young people's developmental needs, we all lose, because those young people become the adults who are responsible for the stewardship of our world. That's why this book is a call to action—a call to get to work on creating a better world for all of us.

Chapter 1: How It Began

Abbey's Story

People called her a great friend. She had deep compassion and empathy for others. She was smart, intelligent, capable, beautiful, sometimes happy, sometimes impulsive, and sometimes sad. At five years old, she worried about the little things.

For example, placing a bottle of water in my purse to bring into the movie theater caused her concern. "What if they find the water?" She wanted to do everything right. She feared doing anything inappropriate or "getting in trouble." This fear was related to "getting in trouble" when she was at her father's house. Eventually, to avoid punishment, she expected nothing less than perfection from herself. This, of course, was an impossible standard to achieve.

One evening, early in March 2012, when she was 21-years-old, Abbey called me crying. She said, "Mom, _____ is acting stupid. Looks like we won't be going through with our plans." She was calm and speaking clearly, so I had no idea how much alcohol she had consumed. Her speech never gave it away.

I asked the typical questions of a concerned mother: "Where are you? Who is with you? Do you want me to come pick you up?"

Her responses told me she was outside a bar, where she and her fiancé were dancing. I said, "Abbey, Mom needs you to go inside. It isn't safe for you to be outside a bar alone."

Our conversation was interrupted when her fiancé found her, and I heard her say to him, "I want to go home." I heard her fiancé, in the background, agree to take her home. Abbey spoke into the phone, addressing me once again.

"Mom, he is going to take me home now."

"Who is the designated driver?"

She gave me the name of her friend and coworker. "Okay. Has he had any alcohol this evening?"

"No," she responded. "We agreed before going out that he was the designated driver."

"Are you sure you don't want me to come pick you up and bring you to Mom's house?"

"No, it's fine, Mom. I'll just go home." "Okay," I said, "Text Mom as soon as you get home, to let me know you are safe."

The last words Abbey spoke before we hung up were, "I love you, Mom" and the last words she texted me, as I slept comfortably in my bed, were "I wish I was dead."

I heard the text about thirty minutes after we hung up. I was in that twilight sleep we parents often inhabit when our children are living at home and out with friends—we are waiting to hear the sound of our child arriving home safely. As I heard the text chime from my phone, I thought, *"She is home safe,"* and I allowed myself to slip into a deep sleep.

A few hours later, I was abruptly awakened. My husband, Abbey's stepfather, was yelling at me, "Kim, get up! There is an emergency. It's Abbey! We must get to the hospital. Hurry!"

I will never forget arriving at the hospital that night. Time slowed as my husband and I followed the signs toward the emergency entrance. Finding a parking place seemed impossible. I was ready to leap from the car and run into the emergency room, but I somehow knew I needed my husband by my side. He parked the car. We ran into the emergency room, only to find that it was extremely busy.

I gave my daughter's name and information to the receptionist behind the glass. He had no idea who I was talking about. He said there was no one with that name in the emergency room.

Finally, after I had described Abbey, and my husband had given the receptionist what limited information he'd gotten from Abbey's fiancé, the receptionist said, "Oh you must be referring to the patient we have listed as Christina Conundrum."

I immediately realized my daughter had been listed as a Jane Doe—meaning she couldn't give her name when she arrived at the hospital. "They're working on her," said the receptionist. "You aren't allowed back there yet."

Having been an X-ray technologist for twenty years, I had a lot of experience with emergency rooms. I immediately knew what "working on her" meant. They were trying to save her life. My worst nightmare had come true. Abbey had been in a horrible accident, and I still didn't have any details.

I felt sick to my stomach. My legs were weak. My heart was beating so fast and so loud I could hear it. I thought it would burst through my chest. It took everything in my power to keep it together. I wanted to shout, "Take me to my daughter! I don't care about your *stupid rules!*" If my daughter was fighting for her life, I wanted to be beside her! But I knew shouting wouldn't get me what I so desperately needed.

I had to keep myself together. I had to stay calm. My internal voice was speaking with deliberate force to keep my body from doing something that would make the hospital call for security. I needed to see my daughter. I needed to know what was happening. I found myself deliberately speaking, with calm and purpose. I began pressing my husband for facts, "What did Abbey's fiancé say when he called the house?"

My husband replied, "All he said was, 'Just hurry and get to the hospital. I'm not there yet. I'm with the police. But you must hurry.'" I returned to the receptionist's window and begged him to let me see my daughter.

"They're still working on her and you can't get in their way."

I was frantic. Desperate. Each moment seemed an eternity. I didn't know what to do with myself. I wanted to run into the back area where I knew I could find Abbey. I worked hard to control myself.

Finally, a nurse approached and asked us to follow her. *Finally*, I thought, *finally, they must have succeeded and now we get to see Abbey.* I was wrong. The nurse led us into a small room—for privacy, I imagine. We followed her. The nurse asked, "Do you have any idea what happened?"

"No!" I replied.

She said, "Your daughter opened the door of the pickup truck where she sat in the passenger seat and hurled herself from the vehicle. The vehicle was going over sixty miles an hour on the freeway. She had high alcohol content in her blood stream. The police are interviewing the others who were in the car with her. You can see her now, but she is unconscious, and I want to prepare you—her eyes are taped shut, and her face, well ..." The nurse hesitated. "We are calling a plastic surgeon to repair her face."

I thought, *If they're calling a plastic surgeon, they must have saved her!* But that moment of hope was shattered as the nurse continued to speak. "Your daughter is on life support. We don't know if she will ever regain consciousness. Time will tell."

"Take me to her," I said.

The nurse began to walk in front of us. I rushed past her and scanned the emergency room. The patients were in neatly organized beds, side by side against the walls. And there she was, just as the nurse had described. She was unconscious. She was on life support. Her eyes were taped shut, but not completely. I begged Abbey, "Wake up. Come back to us." She remained silent, unconscious, lifeless.

Abbey was transferred to the intensive care unit. She was in a coma. There were brain scans. There were tests. Many specialists came to see her. Days passed, and with each additional brain scan, each additional test, and each new examination by a specialist, I hoped, I prayed, and I bargained with God. I told him I would take Abbey's pain. I would trade places with her and lay in a coma for the rest of my life if he would heal her and let her live a full life. But it was never to happen. My tears, my broken heart, my pleas, and my attempts to bargain with God, would not change what came next.

The neurologist wanted to speak with us. "She will never be the girl she once was," he said. "Her brain function is almost completely gone. There is nothing more we can do. If by some small miracle she survives off life support, she will live the rest of her life dependent on others to feed her, change her diapers, and bathe her." Then came the professional suggestion. "She should be removed from life support."

My body was shaking. My stomach was churning. I was nauseas. Fighting back tears. It took every ounce of control to compose myself and deliver a response to the suggestion to remove Abbey's life support.

"What does that mean?" I asked. "What will happen if we remove her life support?" I was confused. I knew I was there in the hospital. I knew exactly what was going on, but my mind couldn't cope with the information it was receiving as fast as the information was being delivered. I had to repeat everything I was hearing from doctors and nurses back to myself, then I had to concentrate on each individual word.

I MUST keep myself under control, I whispered to myself repeatedly. I knew they would sedate me if I lost control. I had to be alert! My mind had to fight my body, but my body was fighting my mind. After Abbey's death I would come to understand a great deal about post-traumatic stress disorder (PTSD).

The neurologist responded, "We know from the limited amount of urine that she is putting out that her lower brainstem isn't functioning, which indicates that without life support, her respiration and heart will fail to function. Removing life support will allow her body to do what comes naturally to it."

I sat in shock and disbelief. My heart was tearing apart. Then more words came out of the doctor's mouth. "Tell us when you are ready to start the procedure."

Days passed. I spoke with more specialists. I had to be sure. I had to be certain. Apparently, Abbey's brain had swelled into her spinal cord. Her brain was damaged beyond repair. I couldn't speak. I couldn't move. People were talking. How could people talk when my baby was just lying there?

How could I agree to remove Abbey from life support? There could be a miracle. Doctors don't know everything. I insisted on more tests. What were the other options? There must be more options! I was confused, overwhelmed, and exhausted when I dropped to my knees and asked God to fill me with love. I was in a fog.

Family and friends were starting to arrive. They were asking questions like, "What happened?" That question was a constant reminder that Abbey had *done this to herself.* She chose this. How could she have done this to herself?

Questions flooded my mind. My child had been at risk for suicide? How did I miss that? Why? Why? Guilt began to consume my mind. Kids with good moms don't commit suicide. I'm a child developmentalist. How could I have missed warning signs of this magnitude?

But for now, these questions had to be pushed into the deep recesses of my mind. I had to be strong for Abbey. This meant there was only one question that needed to be immediately answered.

What could be done to save Abbey's life?

I insisted on speaking with more neurosurgeons. One surgeon suggested a possible course of action—opening Abbey's skull and exposing the brain until the swelling went down. This surgery wouldn't repair the damaged parts of her brain.

Her life would lack any quality. She would be dependent on others for the rest of her life. And there were many obstacles to having any type of cutting-edge surgery. We'd need to find a surgeon willing to perform it and a facility that could support such a drastic procedure. Insurance would need to approve the cost of the procedure and agree to pay for it. I'm a fighter. I felt I could fight to overcome each of these obstacles. But there was more to consider.

Much of Abbey's brain was already damaged beyond repair. The surgery would not restore her to a condition in which she could lead a normal quality of life. She would need twenty-four-hour care for the rest of her life. She might breathe on her own, her heart might keep beating, but she would never, ever have any quality to her life.

I remained in prayer until I knew what had to be done. The day came when I looked at my daughter. I really looked at her—lying in that bed, eyes taped shut, lifeless. I knew in my heart that keeping her in that state was cruel. I also knew that the suggested surgery would not restore Abbey to a life she would want to live. *If* I chose the surgery, *if* I could find a maverick among neurosurgeons to perform it, *if* I could find a facility to support us, *if* I could talk the insurance company into covering the insurmountable costs, or *if* I raised the money myself, the choice would have nothing to do with Abbey's needs. It would be the most selfish and cruel choice I could make. I grappled with thoughts that perhaps God could give us a miracle and the surgery could restore Abbey completely. Then I simply returned to prayer.

Finally, I reached a decision. If Abbey was meant to be healed by God's grace, it would happen through a natural process. I would not try to force God's hand. I would have faith. If Abbey was destined for a miracle, it would happen. My prayer became simple. "God please allow my daughter to find peace, show me the path to lead her to peace, and give me the strength to walk it." I sat next to Abbey's bedside one afternoon, my heart overflowing with love for her. I whispered into her ear, "I'm going to let you go home now, Abbey."

It was the most difficult and painful decision I have ever had to make. And that tortuous decision led to another one. Would I choose life or death for myself? I could remain in life with my living children or I could choose death to end the pain of living in a world without Abbey. But this was a choice for later.

Abbey's biological father and I approved the "procedure." It was done. Her life support was removed. I crawled into her hospital bed. I held her in my arms. I listened with intention to the loud noises that escaped her mouth. She was gasping for air. She was struggling to breathe. All I could do was listen, wait, and wonder when the last gasp would occur.

As I lay beside my dying child, the hustle and bustle of nurses, doctors, and staff continued outside of Abbey's hospital room in the intensive care ward. There was laughter and joking. People were discussing food and lunch or dinner breaks. It was just another day for staff, nurses, and physicians. It was so painful to hear their joy as my child was slowly dying. They were laughing; Abbey was *loudly* gasping for air each and every second of the last fourteen hours of her life. The pain of listening to her was excruciating, particularly with the backdrop of laughter.

We asked the nursing staff to provide more medication to calm Abbey. To relax her further would end her life, they claimed. "But she is dying. Her life *is* ending," I said. "She is suffering."

"She isn't aware of anything," the nurses and doctors assured us. I thought to myself, *how can they possibly know what she is and isn't feeling?* I wasn't comforted by their statements. They had no merit to me. It seemed unreasonable and cruel to allow Abbey to go on and on gasping for air. I was so sad for my child as she lay there so helpless and I cradled her in my arms.

I felt like I was standing in a room full of people, screaming at the top of my lungs, and no-one could hear me. The hospital staff made absurd suggestions about what I might do instead of lying in the bed holding my child as she slowly died. "Have you eaten? You need to eat and keep your strength up. You need to drink water. Have you been drinking water?" Really? *Really?* My daughter is dying and you're suggesting I eat and drink water? Sadness, frustration, anger, and exhaustion gripped my body, my heart, and my soul. I felt like a vice was squeezing my heart—a heart that ached beyond anything I can describe. For years to come I would experience this pain. And, though it comes less frequently, it has never completely left me.

It had been fourteen hours since the *procedure was completed.* Fourteen hours of listening to my daughter grasp for air, until Abbey's final breath. Suddenly, there it was—her final heartbeat. I squeezed her tightly. I listened closely. I was secretly praying for a miracle. I thought her heart would beat again and that the tide would change. I waited in vain. Abbey's heart would never beat again. There was only deafening silence. The tears flowed as I said my good-byes and told her how much I loved her. I was broken.

Perhaps Abbey would never find peace in living. Perhaps her peace could only be found in death. Perhaps only God knew this. In many ways, Abbey's final heartbeat gave her the peace she couldn't find in life. I had tried to bargain with God. I had wanted to trade places with Abbey. I wanted to take her pain and give her a chance to find peace in living. But she found peace in death, and I took on her pain in life. I suppose in some strange way, God gave me what I asked for—just not how I'd intended. I have heard that while we often pray for healing, sometimes healing comes through death. There have been so many times when the pain of losing Abbey has been so profound, so unimaginable that I wished for my own death. I have imagined dozens of ways I would do it.

One year later, a friend of mine faced the same kind of decision. Doctors told her that she needed to remove her mother from life support. She called me, asking for advice. "How did you do it?" she asked. "How were you able to decide to remove Abbey's life support?"

I replied, "I had to love her so completely and so unselfishly that I could say goodbye. I had to give her what she needed, which was peace." This was my truth. But living with one's truth can cause great pain.

After Abbey's death, I retreated into the darkest places of my mind. My whole world went black. I could not find peace, and I found it impossible to move into the light.

I lay in the bed beneath the covers, unable to leave my room. Friends and family came to support me, but most days I refused to see anyone. It hurt too much. I knew my friends were trying to support me. But truthfully, I knew being with them would cause me unbearable pain. Looking at them would remind me that their families were intact. Their children were all alive, and one of mine was dead. I felt guilty even having these thoughts, being jealous of friends with living children. I certainly didn't want any of them to lose a child just so that they could understand my pain. Still, there was the awful, gnawing feeling that my friends and family could bring me no comfort because their children were alive.

There was another fight happening inside me. Should I live, or should I die? If I died, I could find Abbey. I could hold her again—I could hold her and never let go. But I'd be leaving my other children behind.

My children might believe I loved Abbey more than I loved them, which wasn't true. I didn't want to abandon them. I only wanted to abandon my pain and find Abbey. Yet, to do so would be a one-way trip. My children would be left to mourn their mother and their sister. I could not make a decision that would harm any of my living children.

Consequently, there was a constant internal battle in my mind—how could I end my unbearable pain without harming my living children? There was no escaping this seemingly unending, internal battle. I frequently begged God to let me die. This way, the pain could end, but I wouldn't be responsible for taking my own life. I would stare at train tracks while sitting in my car and silently think to myself: *If a train came by, I could just run out in front of it and end all this anguish and struggle.*

Sleep, when it was possible, brought moments of peace. But when I awoke, I was forced to remember ... Abbey died. All that was possible while she lived was now impossible. I wouldn't see her happy again. I wouldn't see her married. I wouldn't see her become a mother. It was all so definite, so final. Every dream, hope, and vision for her future was gone.

Mother's Day came two months after Abbey took her last breath. I wanted to disappear. I wanted the day to *stop!* I took one antianxiety pill after another in hopes that time could just stop. I took so many I almost got my wish, because I overdosed. My heart stopped. Later, I was told that my husband had performed CPR (cardiac resuscitation) and called an ambulance. An emergency paramedic continued to work on me until we reached the hospital.

When I regained consciousness, I immediately noticed a security guard in the doorway of the private emergency room where I lay—apparently, they were there to stop me from hurting myself. I wasn't trying to end my life. I just needed to stop time. I needed *everything* to stop. But nobody believed me when I told them so. Eventually, they transferred me to a *behavioral management center*—which, in medical terms, is code for "mental institution." I went on to have a complete nervous breakdown. It took a long time before I could start getting better.

Since then, my journey back has been long and arduous. I freely admit, I'm not the woman I once was. I never made it back to those days when I believed in a "happily ever after." Those were childhood dreams.

A close friend told me that no one ever cries themselves to death. It was her sweet way of giving me permission to cry as much and as often as I needed. Yet, I realized one thing: perhaps we can't cry ourselves to death, but we can surely cry our lives away. I was standing at a precipice. I had to choose whether I wanted to live, die, or cry my life away.

I chose to live. I chose it for the sake of my other children. But I needed to figure out how to go about it. Using antianxiety medication to numb the pain would *not* be a choice to live. I had to find a way to heal. I had to understand what had happened, and *why* it happened. Only then could I decide what to do about it all. I was forced to look back and face the truth. And I did this hoping that the truth would help the healing begin.

Abbey was kind, caring, intelligent, empathetic, and loyal. She had a strong sense of responsibility. She was beautiful inside and outside. She always spoke up for the underdog. She disliked unkind behavior.

Abbey also expected perfection from herself. She agonized over mistakes, or what she perceived to be failures. Despite my attempts to calm her, she would get so angry with herself that she would beat her head against the bathtub. Her therapist explained that Abbey suffered from posttraumatic stress disorder (PTSD) as a result of a stressful and traumatic childhood.

Abbey's childhood was fraught with custody battles between her father and me. There were endless appointments with court-ordered mediators. There were forced visitations to a home very different from my own. Abbey was threatened, teased, and ignored for long hours. Her sister was told not to talk to her during visitations, because Abbey had wet the bed and she was a "pee-pee baby."

Abbey endured horrendous psychological abuse. Years and years passed during which I tried to use the flawed family court system to protect her and, at that time, my one other child. But those years were filled with unending terror for Abbey and her sister. As I began to search for answers, I discovered that I had some false beliefs about how all of this would impact my children.

A MOTHER'S DISCOVERY

Most adults, including me, believe that children are resilient and that they recover from stress and trauma easily. But this is a false belief. Children are not equally resilient. Like Abbey, they don't all recover. The court system also doesn't recognize the effects of psychological abuse on a child's brain development. It doesn't acknowledge that from the moment an infant is born and throughout their developing years they are learning about themselves, who they are, and whether they matter to the adults they interact with daily. This means that a young person's self-image is overwhelmingly influenced by how the adults in their life respond to them and behave toward them. The family court system has one goal in mind—to reunite parents with their children even at the cost of inadvertently destroying a child's development.

Inappropriately behaved parents are given countless opportunities to learn good parenting skills. This makes children the guinea pigs in an experiment to see whether these parents can get their act together. Later in this book, we will explore the family situations that are leaving deeply scarred hearts and negative self-images across our nation and the world. These are situations which never make it into our court system, but which nevertheless harm our youth by failing to support and promote a positive self-image. In fact, during my research for this book I was shocked to discover how many kids in the US are victims of stressful and traumatic circumstances; circumstances which keep them from developing a positive self-image and becoming productive and happy adults.

These are circumstances you'd recognize if I pointed them out. You'd probably even consider them "normal." For example, most of us don't think of perfectionism as something dangerous. Some of us even wear it as a badge of honor. But, from a clinical standpoint, children like Abbey strive for perfection in hopes of earning love from those who matter most to them. They desperately need this love so they can feel okay or worthy. They need it so they can find a sense of connection and significance. Abbey always had to have a boyfriend. If she could please him, if she could be perfect enough and if he was happy with her, she could feel loved and safe. But when these relationships became challenging, her PTSD kicked in and it kicked in hard. All the negative feelings rose up within her, leaving her feeling worthless and unlovable.

As I faced the truth, I began to understand why Abbey threw herself from a moving vehicle. But there was much more that I needed to explore. There had to be a concrete and scientific explanation beyond the mere "low self-esteem" argument. I was still having a hard time understanding why my loving and positive parenting behaviors hadn't influenced Abbey's beliefs about herself. Why didn't my parenting override the horrible behaviors of her other parent?

Through my research, I discovered the profound effect stress and trauma have on brain development—including the limbic system which is the seat of our emotions, and the frontal lobe which we use to make rational judgments.

Emotionally healthy people use the frontal lobe to decide how to respond to their emotions. But emotionally unhealthy people do not make the connection between these two areas of the brain. Instead, they are ruled by their emotions—particularly when they are upset or feel threatened or challenged. If you have ever witnessed someone "flying off the handle in anger" or "flipping their lid when they are mad" you're watching someone who, in that moment, is operating from their limbic system.

When we operate from our limbic system, without engaging our frontal lobe, we shut down the reasoning factors which we'd normally use to control ourselves. Many of us can get angry and fly off the handle at times. But people with healthy brain development rarely do. And even when they do, they have an easier time regaining control.

This is because healthy brain development helps the pre-frontal cortex (the reasoning mind) to rule over the limbic system (the emotional mind). People with this ability have more control over their emotions and impulses, not because they're less emotional, but because their reasoning mind is in control. People whose brains don't develop in this way can go from appearing normal and in control, to being completely ruled by their emotions. Sometimes, the shift is so sudden and so dramatic, it's like you're talking to a different person.

Through my research, I began to understand that Abbey sometimes functioned from her limbic system (emotions) and from her brain stem (survival). When she was in challenging or threatening situations, it took very little to provoke her. She often acted spontaneously, without forethought—a common behavior for children who have traumatic experiences early in life. Though it's true that she had occasional suicidal thoughts, she had always been able to share those feelings with me. We'd talk about how she would not go through with it because she knew how sad it would make me. At those times, she could think through the consequences of her actions by using her prefrontal cortex. She could own her feelings while also understanding how her actions would impact others.

On the day of her suicide, Abbey had spent time doing ordinary things. She got a manicure and pedicure and was looking forward to an evening with her fiancé. She and I had scheduled some time together to shop for wedding venues on the following day. But I believe, on that fateful evening, she found herself in the middle of a perfect storm. Between the alcohol, the fight with her fiancé, and the opportunity to jump out of the truck, she became ruled by emotion and by her need to escape it all. Her response was not a choice. It was a spontaneous reaction.

I'd finally discovered some answers, some truth. But could these answers help me heal? After many sleepless nights and endless bouts of crying and sadness, I now realize that I will never completely heal. But I know that I can get to a better, healthier place. Each day *I remind myself that on the other side of grief and madness, there is love and hope.*

A Mother's Decision

When I made my choice to live, I decided to commit myself to my three daughters—two living, Emily and Mandi, and one dead, Abbey. I decided to live the rest of my life honoring what I learned from Abbey's death. I committed myself to the young people who call me mom, and to their children who sweetly refer to me as Grandma and "Dr. Grandma." I call them my "heart children." My love for them and their love for me has kept me grounded in the world of the living. It has supported my work in writing this book, in building *Abbey's Purple Winged Angels Foundation*, and in developing *Dr. Kim's XtraOrdinary Youth*.

Deep inside, I know it's the best way I can honor Abbey's life—to commit myself, my work, and my efforts to protecting other children from the damage caused by childhood trauma. The heart of my vision is to save lives, to change the negative, pessimistic thinking that robs young people of their goals and dreams, and to replace it with positive, optimistic thinking habits and behaviors. This is my mission, to empower young people to live—*ExtraOrdinary Lives!*

WHAT THIS BOOK WILL DO FOR YOU

The first thing this book will do for you is help you find the Abbeys in *your* life. As a child development specialist, it's my job to understand the best parenting, discipline, and communication styles. But I also used them. I thought they would help Abbey reach her full potential. Yes, Abbey was a sensitive child. She didn't adapt to change easily. But that didn't explain her suicide. It was hard to grasp what drove Abbey to take her own life, especially in the way she did and for a reason that *seemed* benign.

But Abbey's death drove me to discover how dramatically self-image shapes our thinking and behavior. It motivated me to learn why so many young people are at risk for building a poor self-image, and what we can do to make a difference. I want

28

to emphasize that a poor self-image is not only destructive to our development; it has the power to destroy lives.

In the preface of this book, I said that young people like Abbey are not typically viewed as "at risk." They behave appropriately, they have friends, they are loved, they love others, they do well in school, they laugh, they joke, they come from good homes, and they seem to have all their needs met. But there's a hidden danger for children like Abbey, and even the most vigilant parents can miss it.

Young people like Abbey are what I call "invisible kids." Not because people don't notice them, but because even the adults who interact with them daily do not recognize them as "at risk." This makes invisible children *more* at risk because they do not get what they really need. Think of an invisible kid as a person paddling down the river in a canoe, with a steep 100 foot drop just ahead of them—only they can't see it.

There's no telling what will happen once they reach the drop. Sometimes, the drop isn't even sudden. Abbey's "drop" was her suicide. Other invisible kid's may choose other self-harming behaviors to deal with their pain. Some kids are in so much pain that they will hurt others. Behind all these behaviors, is an invisible menace that no one sees, because they never think of these children as being "at risk."

In an upcoming chapter, we'll discuss the various behaviors young people use to replace the consistent "meaningful connections" they need. These connections are meant to help them cope with challenges, and to form a positive self-image.

Invisible children don't get these connections. Even when the parent is doing everything they can to provide them. Sometimes, it's the invisible needs that really matter. Childhood stress and trauma is what causes these needs to go into hiding. This is more common than most adults realize. In later chapters, I think you'll be shocked (just as I was) to discover why almost 50 percent of children living in the US experience stress and trauma during childhood. Likewise, 60 percent of adults with physical and mental illnesses report that they were victims of stress and trauma during childhood. Physical and mental illness are related to childhood stress and trauma.

Dr. Vincent Felitti's study of seventeen thousand middle-class Americans documented that adverse childhood experiences (ACEs) clearly contribute significantly to negative adult physical and mental health outcomes and affect more than 60 percent of adults. Klebanov and Travis (2015) quote Dr. Felitti:

"Adverse childhood experiences are common, destructive, and have an effect that often lasts for a lifetime. They are the most important

determinant of the health and well-being of our nation."

Bottom line, there are a lot more "Abbeys" out there than you think. That's why **the first thing this book will do for you** is help you find the Abbeys in your life.

- Do you have an Abbey living in your home?
- Do you have a family member or relative who is an Abbey?
- Do you have an Abbey in your classroom or where you volunteer?
- Do you tutor, mentor, or coach an Abbey?
- Do your kids have a friend like Abbey?
- Do you provide spiritual guidance to an Abbey?

It's likely that you answered yes to at least one of these questions. If not, I'm pretty sure you will by the end of this book. Again, there are more Abbey's out there than you realize. **To reach them, you must make meaningful connections with the young people in your life whenever it is possible.** This is why, **the second thing this book will do for you** is teach you the habit of building meaningful connections.

I'd define a meaningful connection as one which intentionally promotes the development of a positive self-image and of good communication skills. This is easier than it sounds, but like anything else, it can be deliberately learned and mastered. When these connections happen, they give a young person everything they need to live a happy and fulfilling life. They also ensure adult-to-youth relationships that are grounded in trust, respect and compassion. When these connections don't happen, the young person's needs go unmet, and they become another invisible kid.

Some teachers, coaches, or other caregivers and educators assume it's not their responsibility to build meaningful connections with young people. Their plates are full. They have their own children to worry about. But when building meaningful connections becomes a habitual part of your parenting/care-taking, communication, and discipline style it will feel just as natural as any of your everyday behaviors.

Adults that use meaningful connections, including myself, find that in the long run we save time and energy by helping youth develop better thinking habits. First, because these connections support the development of a positive self-image. Second, they encourage brain development which connects the young person's frontal lobe with their limbic system. This makes a person's higher, reasoning mind the master of their reactionary emotional mind. In the long run, this makes meaningful connecting a much more efficient strategy, even for busy adults.

Young people who don't have meaningful relationships with adults (abused, neglected children or those living in foster care) are at risk for depression, anxiety, "learned helplessness," self-harm (e.g., drug and alcohol use), suicide and for harming others by gun violence etc. These young people will

32

become adults living with these same issues. What will that mean for their children, communities, nations—or for our world?

This is why this book is a call to action—whether you are a parent or guardian of a young person or whether you work with young people in some other way, you can make a huge difference in their lives! So again, **the second thing this book will do for you** is teach you the habit of building meaningful connections. If building meaningful connections seems hard and time-consuming, it's because you're not in the habit of doing it. Once it becomes a habit, building meaningful connections will be much, much easier and natural—even fun.

The third thing this book will do for you is show you how self-image and meaningful connections work together to help a young person become a "whole person." Young people who are not whole grow up to live frustrating and even chaotic lives. They might have streaks of success and happiness—sometimes lasting several years. But they'll also experience long or recurring bouts with self-sabotage, sadness, frustration or even depression. They might spend years building a great career, marriage or friendship, only to flush it all away in weeks, days, hours or even minutes by making a few impulsive or selfish decisions.

I know there are a lot of self-help books that talk about "becoming whole." But most of them deal in gooey abstractions that leave you with no practical course of action. This book is written from the perspective of an educational developmental scientist (EDS) who has a deep understanding of human development. Through my personal tragedy, and my responses to it, I've learned how this knowledge can help you make a difference for the Abbeys in your life.

Educational developmental psychology uses a human developmental lens to study how people learn. We also focus on age appropriate research and strategies. I think we'll agree that a five-year-old has different skills and challenges than a ten-year-old and that they learn differently. Most importantly, developmental psychology takes a *whole person* approach when exploring, considering, or discussing the different needs and skills of an individual and how those needs, and skills affect learning.

By *whole person* I mean the full integration of the *five selves*:

- The cognitive self
- The creative self
- The emotional self
- The social self
- The physical self

These five "selves" make up the mosaic of your self-image. Together, they shape your thinking habits and your life. The critical, often neglected point, is that self-image and the five "selves" are deeply intertwined and dependent on one another. A need deprived in one of them, can cause an imbalance that upsets the development of the others. This is how unmet needs make it nearly impossible for some youth to persist in their learning or even to concentrate long enough to learn a new skill. This is why, as a developmental scientist, I will focus on:

- The development of self-image, including the five selves;

- The intellectual, creative, emotional, social, and physical needs; and

- Age appropriate learning strategies that bring out a young person's unique abilities.

These strategies help a young person develop a healthy self-image, by developing the full "mosaic" of their five selves. So again, **the third thing this book will do for you** is show you how self-image and meaningful connections work together to help a young person become a *whole person*.

The fourth thing this book will do for you is give you the tools to help young people discover their creative genius by tapping into their natural talents and learning how to use them to serve others. Norman Cousins said, *"Death is not the greatest loss in life. The greatest loss is what dies inside us while we live."* Would it surprise you to learn that adolescents who discover their creative genius are much more likely to become happy and productive adults? Of course, it wouldn't. Sadly, too many people either never discover and/or never develop their natural talents. Because of this, they never tap into their most abundant source of happiness and significance—the one inside them.

Traditional education is focused on the intellectual and physical needs—either through extracurricular activities or study programs. But the creative, social and emotional needs often go unmet. Of course, schools can only do so much. They're overwhelmed with a large population of diverse young people from a wide variety of home conditions. They must teach curriculum under tight time constraints—so they need students to behave in a way that makes this possible. Sports and all other recreational activities are much the same. They focus on training or preparing students to excel in a specific athletic area, but they face the same timing and operational constraints. Of course, some young people get their creative, social and emotional needs met at home. But young people, like Abbey, have these needs met in some environments, only to have them neglected or even destabilized in others.

Sadly, some young people, particularly adolescents, are not getting any of their creative, social or emotional needs met. This means, they miss out on connecting with their creative needs and their social needs, both of which are essential to their self-image and their ability to find their natural genius. Becoming extraordinary requires getting outside the boundaries of the ordinary. This takes creativity. Most importantly, it takes social sensitivity and emotional maturity. Even the most creative ideas will never get off the ground if they don't do something to make people's lives better. If a young person discovers a skill or a talent, but they never find a way to use that talent to meet other people's needs, they'll never be able to turn that talent into a meaningful vocation.

But an idea that genuinely makes people's lives better can change the world and fill life with happiness and meaning the likes of which some people only dream of. This is how people discover their true vocation in life, instead of just settling for a career they think will make them money. When you find your creative genius, what you are naturally good at, you're productive and joyful. You feel like a significant member of humanity.

But it takes more than talent to make this happen. It also takes social and emotional skills. Many very talented people sabotage opportunities because they can't express their needs in a healthy way or empathize with others. But if you develop emotional skills like self-regulation, you can stop and consider outcomes before you act. This makes it more likely that your needs will be met. But it also assures that you'll be able to empathize with others, make friends and use your talents to serve others by meeting their needs. This is why emotional development is an important part of discovering your creative genius and finding your place in society. When you accomplish this, you know that you are a worthy member of the human race. But it all starts when we're young. That's why the adults in a young person's life must provide opportunities for the young person to develop these crucial life skills. So again, **the fourth thing this book will do for you** is give you the tools to help young people discover their creative genius by tapping into their natural talents.

The fifth and final thing this book will do for you is show you how to become such a force of influence in young people's lives, that you won't have to wait on the "right" politicians to be elected or the "right" policies to give our kids the kind of world we want them to inherit. Have you wondered why so many of our citizens, including famous and wealthy citizens, are so unhappy? Have you wondered why so many young people and adults choose behaviors that remove them from reality to reduce their stress and anxiety?

Why are so many people choosing social media, excessive gaming, antidepressants, excessive marijuana use, alcohol, and even violence to feel or not to feel at all? Why are so many of our citizens violent, angry, joining gangs, or committing crimes against innocent people? Why do so many of us consume endlessly to "be happy" for fleeting moments until we need another "happiness fix?" Why would we rather sit at a dinner table with family and friends and have our heads downturned looking at our cell phones? Why are we afraid to talk with a stranger while in line, or on an elevator? Why are our electronic devices safer, easier, and more alluring compared to another human being? Why are so many people marching to jobs that bring them no joy—or that they even hate? And why are we forcing our youth to do the same thing?

Yet, despite all these problems, have you ever wondered why our country, like many other nations, judges the health of the nation on the gross domestic product (GDP) rather than the self-images, intellectual, creative, emotional, social, and physical health of our citizens? I think we'll agree that all the problems I just listed have more to do with these "intangible" values.

If our political system doesn't care about the emotional well-being of our young people and our citizens shouldn't we as human beings seek to change that? We can start by asking the right questions of our young people. For example, as adults we push youth to find careers that will make them a lot of money. We do not ask them, "What type of experiences do you want to have in your everyday life?" If we asked them this question, they would use their natural talents and interests to figure out what they wanted to do to make money. This way, they would earn money and happiness at the same time, instead of earning money at the expense of their happiness.

I think we'll agree that no nation can be productive, meaningful and joyful if it fails to raise its youth to pursue productive, meaningful, and joyful vocations. But would you agree, that succeeding in this area, would make any nation such a happy and healthy place, that people would no longer feel the need to sell out their true callings just to earn enough money to buy more "stuff?" This raises an exciting challenge for all adults. First, we must know who the Abbey's in our life really are. Second, we must make a habit of building meaningful connections with them. Third, we must help them grow up to be whole people with positive self-images. Fourth, we must empower them to discover their creative genius by tapping into their natural talents.

So again, **the fifth and final thing this book will do for you** is show you how to become such a force of influence in young people's lives, that you won't have to wait on the "right" politicians to be elected or the "right" policies to give our kids the kind of world we want them to inherit. Imagine, you could become the adult who does this for the Abbey's in your life—and that's our final goal for this book.

THE CORE ISSUE: SELF-IMAGE

Self-image is the GPS that guides you through life. If you've used a GPS, you know they can either be wonderful, or worthless. When your GPS guides you wrong, you end up lost, late or both. When it guides you right, you find your destination with no trouble at all, even if you're in a completely unfamiliar town, city, state or country. The one difference is that your GPS can never guide you completely off the road, into a building or off a cliff. But a negative or distorted self-image can create comparable disasters in your life, even without your conscious permission.

The technical definition of self-image is your belief about your abilities, appearance, personality, and about the roles you play in your family, your workplace and/or your community. Think of your self-image as a magic mirror that reflects your beliefs about who you are. If you see yourself as ugly, it reflects ugly, even if you're very attractive. But your self-image also reflects your "invisible" qualities, like your intellectual and emotional skills. If you see yourself as highly intelligent, your self-image reflects high-intelligence, even if you're only of average intelligence. The same is true with your physical abilities, your emotional maturity, your social skills and even your beliefs about what you do and don't deserve.

Self-image doesn't "reflect" who you really are. It reflects your beliefs about who you are. This is how your self-image shapes your thinking, your judgments, your decisions, and your behaviors. It determines whether you use and develop the skills and talents you have, and it determines when and how much you'll use them. For example, a positive self-image drives you to persist when you're challenged because it "sees" you as someone who deserves the success that you're after. This is even true when you consciously doubt your own abilities, or when you're depressed, or even when you feel hopeless. A positive self-image will inspire you to press on despite these conscious insecurities because it assures you that you *can* succeed and that you *deserve* to succeed. Likewise, a negative self-image will drive you to give up at the first signs of resistance, because—whether you're consciously aware of it or not, it "sees" you as being incapable or even undeserving.

Imagine trying to navigate through an unfamiliar territory with a faulty GPS. That's what it's like to live with a negative or misguided self-image. Your self-image starts taking shape in childhood, and it's shaped by the messages you receive from adults—whether you like the adults or not. Therefore, as adults, we need to be careful about using put downs to shape a young person's behavior. They might not have the intellectual capacity to resist the message, and their brain will accept it as real. Given enough time, we can't blame a young person if they start acting exactly like the words we've put into their heads.

It doesn't matter if the words are in the form of commands either. Saying "don't be stupid," just affirms to a young person that they're being stupid. If they hear this enough, they'll start to believe that they *are* stupid. And if a young person believes they are stupid, useless, or a mess, why should they strive to be anything else? Think of this like programming your GPS. You can program it to have a completely backwards, inside out "map" of the city you're in, and you'll always be lost and wondering why nothing works out for you the way it does for everyone else. Likewise, the messages children hear from the adults remain "programmed" deep within their subconscious—whether the messages are true or not.

Many of these children become so accustomed to these negative or distorted messages, the messages become impossible to ignore or even to consciously detect. If you have "bad" habits, that you can't seem to break even to save your life, you're probably being influenced by similar messages.

Self-harming behaviors such as alcoholism and drug abuse, including excessive marijuana use, excessive gaming, excessive use of technology and social media, being harmful (physically or verbally) to others, bullying, and aggression

—all of these are directly linked to a misguided self-image. On the other hand, people who feel good about themselves believe they can live the lives they choose to live. They believe in themselves, and they believe they have control over their destiny. Most importantly, because they do not see themselves as helpless and because they feel in control of their lives, they don't use self-harming behaviors or inflict harm on others just to prove that they have power over something.

Now, think about the Abbey's in your life. How is self-image driving their thinking and behaviors? Most important, is the GPS of their self-image driving them directly down a dead-end road, or even off a cliff? I am now convinced that self-image is the core issue that drove Abbey to suicide. Her self-image was dependent on what others saw, what others said, and what others did in reaction to her. The evening of her suicide, Abbey's feelings were about the fight with her fiancé and those feelings were magnified and distorted by the alcohol. But all this exacerbated her misguided self-image. Desperate for a way out of the immediate situation, it guided her in a deadly direction.

A misguided self-image isn't always a case of literal life and death. But if you consider how easy it is to waste precious years of your life taking wrong turns, driving down dead end roads and recovering from head on collisions, I think we'll agree that your self-image is something you should protect and care for as much as you care for any of your vital organs. That's why this book takes a deep dive into self-image.

We'll talk about what self-image is and what it isn't. We'll talk about why it's so important for your well-being and, most important, what causes some people to form a negative or misguided self-image while others build healthy and positive ones.

A WORD ON SAVING LIVES

Can a healthy self-image save a young person's life? In my research—which you'll find in the bonus chapters of this book—I've discovered several issues that rob young people of a positive self-image. If I had to summarize all these issues, I'd say it boils down to how young people respond to stress and trauma. To be more precise, it happens when a young person's need for meaningful connections with adults goes unmet for too many of their developmental years. Therefore, to save lives, adults must build connections that:

- Move young people away from depression, anxiety, and away from numbing their sense of helplessness by using narcotics (legal or illegal), alcohol, and/or attempted suicide.

- Move young people away from behaviors which drive them to "just feel something" in unhealthy ways (e.g., self-mutilation, cutting, promiscuity, etc.).

- Move young people away from excessive video gaming, social media, technology, etc. and toward real-world meaningful connections. These behaviors might not be "bad," but they're often a substitute for meaningful connections.

With respect to building a positive self-image, young people must have opportunities to explore, discover, make mistakes, try again, master new concepts, master new skills, master new behaviors, develop their natural talents, and explore their own interests. When young people get these opportunities through meaningful connections, a natural and positive self-image emerges and with that self-image comes the positive thinking habits that will change their life.

Too many kids never get this opportunity—especially from the adults in their lives. Instead, their home life, school life and their community life are all filled with frustrating challenges that leave them feeling helpless. These young people need every adult on board making meaningful connections with them. They need adults to show them that they're important, that they matter, that they're valuable that they have something special to give to the world and that they're profoundly significant as a member of society. This takes work and patience on the part of the adult. Developing a positive self-image is a process, and it doesn't happen overnight. Most important, it takes a commitment that starts in the mind and it really does take a village of adults to make it happen. There is a saying:

"We cannot know from whom or from where the next great leap for mankind comes."

Any one of the Abbey's in your life could be the next great diplomat, entrepreneur, inventor, doctor, counselor, law-maker, judge, or spiritual teacher. All that is possible while they live could be made real by the impact you have on their lives. Our greatest challenges can only be solved if the minds of every day men and women are deeply engaged. If we do our part, even in the little things, we never know what kind of a ripple we will send through our society.

Please join me in becoming part of our community—a community that recognizes young people as our greatest resource.

Chapter 2: The Conflicted, Yet Heartfelt Journey of Caregivers

'Oy Vey!'

From the moment an infant is born, nurses and physicians must check the newborn's coloring, respiration, muscle tone, activity, and heartbeat. New parents anxiously check to make sure their baby is healthy—even up to counting their fingers and toes. This is the beginning of the heartfelt, yet conflicted journey of a caregiver.

Most caregivers really want to do their best. It's

How many ways can I say 'overwhelm'?

our job. We must prepare young people for life. We want them to do well in school because we realize that academic excellence increases their career choices. We want them to develop social and emotional skills because we understand that these skills make them more successful in social environments. We also realize that young people's social and emotional skills underscore all their relationships *and* help them navigate life in socially acceptable ways. We want to teach our young people effective coping skills because we know they'll face challenges, obstacles, and uncertainty.

We spend hours picking perfect car seats to take them home from the hospital safely. If we don't breastfeed, we research the best formulas. We read baby food labels to make certain we're meeting their nutritional needs. We buy mobiles for their cribs, so they'll develop good eyesight. We buy infant toys to aid them in grasping and exploring—books for listening and reading. We give them lots of "floor time" to promote sitting, crawling, and walking. We buy the perfect-sized potty seats, and pull-up pants to encourage independent toileting. We spend hours selecting the perfect set of tiny eating utensils, and the perfectly-sized (and decorated) sippy cups. All this to prepare them for the joyous day when they can say, "Look at me—I did it all by myself!"

As our infants reach preschool years, we buy more advanced toys, games, and books to prepare them for school. In a short time, they're proudly singing the alphabet and counting to ten for Grandma and Grandpa or, identifying basic shapes and colors.

A few years after they're born, we send them into the world of formal education. And whether we're the parent, relative, teacher, or friend, our hearts break every time we see our young people suffer teasing, bullying, failure, or rejection. It's hard for any caregiver to accept that they can't protect a child whom they love from the reality of living in the world.

As our children become teens, they start to discover that their caregivers aren't perfect. They realize that we don't have all the answers. And as we fall from the pedestals they put us on during the early years of their lives, we realize that teens can be very hard on us about it.

I remember my teen showing me a picture of myself from ten years earlier and saying, "I want this mom back." I laughed and replied, "I want her back too. She was thinner, with fewer wrinkles!" She didn't find my comment entertaining! She threw the photo down and stormed off, yelling, "I'm serious, Mom!"

As our teens become young adults, we become their encouragers and their advisers. We talk to them about school, sex, money, friendships, and career choices. Sometimes, they want to talk about things we're unprepared to hear, saying things like:

- "I'm failing my class."

- "I'm pregnant."
- "I got someone pregnant."
- "I'm gay."
- "I think I'm trapped in the wrong body."
- "I was suspended from school"
- "I was caught cheating on an exam."
- "I was caught stealing."
- "I'm depressed."
- "Something is wrong with me, but I don't know what it is."
- "I hate myself."
- "I hate you!"
- "I think I'm just going to kill myself."
- "I wish I were dead."
- "I thought about killing myself."

We could list dozens more, but the point is that it's impossible to predict what our young person might bring to us.

ALL WE DO IN THE NAME OF LOVE

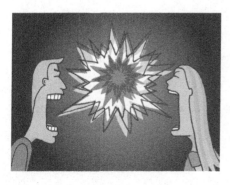 In the years between their birth and adulthood, we cheer our young people on, scold them, hug them, punish them, calm them, discipline them, talk to them, lecture them, and use

time-ins and time-outs. We reason with them, debate them, argue our points of view with them, explain things to them, encourage them, discourage them, and sometimes move between yelling at them and simply ignoring them. We do all this with unconditional love in our heart, managing every situation the best way we know how.

When we're faced with issues involving our youth, regardless of their age, we seek advice from friends or from our own parents. We read books to find solutions. We look for answers on the Internet. Sometimes, we explore products and programs that advertise the "best" solution. With so much information coming from so many directions, and from so many sources, how do we know which information is accurate and which is best suited for our child's needs?

In summary, from the moment our children are born, we're searching for ways to help them live healthy, independent adult lives. But young people face a variety of issues as they move through their developmental years. While some of these issues are unexpected, and almost all of them are unplanned, we do our best to address them as they come.

Is there a way to be more proactive, instead of managing each issue in the moment? How can we better prepare ourselves and our youth to cope with life's unexpected circumstances? We can do it by giving them opportunities and experiences that will help them manage their own challenges. We can help them use self-regulation and self-control to think before they act, and to make the best choice, even in the most unexpected circumstances.

I think we'll agree that how we respond to unexpected events is more important than how we respond to expected ones. I've yet to meet anyone who lost control of their life because of something they *expected* to happen. Likewise, some of the greatest opportunities come to us by ways and means that are totally unexpected. This is why it's so important to learn principle-based strategies that will help our young people assess situations, make good choices, act on those choices, and follow through with consistency and commitment.

WARNING: NATURAL RESISTANCE

Most of us are resistant to learning better ways to interact with our children. We assume that once we become parents, a special knowledge jumps into our brains and that we instantly know what's best for our youth. Our culture doesn't put a lot of value on such training either. We only make it a priority when a crisis comes up—such as in the case of child abuse or neglect. In fact, we require more training to drive a vehicle than we do to raise and to care for young people. Many politicians add to this problem with statements like: "Government needs to get out of the way of parents because parents know what's best for their children"—and the crowds cheer!

When I hear things like this, I think: *Really? Do we trust immature parents, abusive parents, parents with inaccurate developmental knowledge, pedophiles, murderers, rapists, gang members, alcoholics, drug addicts, and mentally ill people to know what's best for their kids? Can we trust these types of parents to model appropriate behaviors and to provide appropriate learning opportunities to their children?*

For a long time, our society has embraced the well-researched facts about early learning and its influence on overall development, with no awareness of what the research really means. For example, we acknowledge that early childhood education has a significant and positive impact on a youngster's early learning. We also acknowledge that early learning has a critical impact on their later learning. But most people don't know that *high-quality* early childhood education (from birth to eight years old), calls for teachers to focus on the needs and skills of the whole child. Although research reveals significant net gains in learning as a result of the whole person approach, this approach is still not used in educational settings for age groups older than eight. I consider this a travesty because when adolescents do not get all their needs met, they can fall through the cracks, get off track, and again we all lose.

- The *whole person* teaching approach produces the best learning environment for young people and therefore the best learning outcomes for everyone.

- *Whole person* teaching is based on meeting a young person's intellectual, creative, emotional, social, and physical needs, and on helping them develop skills for meeting these needs on their own.

- The *whole person* approach calls for teachers to make meaningful connections when interacting with youth. These meaningful connections are steeped in evidence-based strategies for building positive self-image, self-regulation, self-control, positive self-esteem, and a strong sense of self-efficacy, resulting in greater self-confidence.

- The *whole person* approach recognizes that young people of the same age vary in their needs and skills. This is important because the success of skill development depends on the quality of the learning opportunities provided to youth.

Regarding the final point above, not all five-year-olds have been given the same opportunities to develop a specific skill. This is why, despite being the same age, skill levels will vary from child to child. This is true for all young people as well as adults. We often meet people of the same age whose intellectual, creative, emotional, social, and physical skills are very different. Their self-image and the pillars of their self-image vary as well. This is because they have all had varying learning opportunities throughout their developmental years. Remember, we learn to think negatively or positively about ourselves depending on the opportunities and experiences adults provide us with during our development.

Imagine the skills and self-image development of a five-year-old who attended a high-quality early childhood education program, from birth to the age of five, while her parents were away at work. How would her skills and self-image compare to a five-year-old who attended a substandard early childhood education program, or a five-year-old who did not attend an early childhood education? The skills of these children would be very different if the other care they received did not use the *whole person* teaching approach.

Now imagine what will happen when these three children enter kindergarten or first grade. Which child will be able to build friendships with peers and establish a positive relationship with their teacher? Who will be more successful in their school work? How will their successes (or their failures) affect their self-image and the pillars of their self-image? How about for the child who has *not* had this kind of training? Some children begin their formal education with the skills they need to succeed, and some do not. The children who do not, are the children who most need the *whole person* teaching approach. Yet they are unlikely to get it after third grade. As the needs of the *whole person* continue to go unmet, children's behaviors become more disruptive, and teachers and parents become more frustrated. This is how the vicious cycle begins, and as it continues, the child falls further behind in their education and social development.

Working parents spend a lot of money on early childhood education to give their child a good place to go during the workday. The problem is that most parents cannot afford *high-quality* early childhood education. Some childcare institutions boast that their programs *are* quality early childhood education programs, but this doesn't mean they employ Master Level Credentialed Teachers. Such teachers have the appropriate training to address the needs and skills of the *"whole child."* The problem is, these teachers require higher salaries than teachers employed by state-funded schools. Parent's tuition fees often aren't enough to pay for these salaries.

The US government recognizes that high-quality early education is a real game changer, which is why they fund Head Start for impoverished families. However, the working poor and middle-class Americans who pay for childcare are limited to what fits their already airtight budget. High-quality early education can easily cost $1,700 to 2,800 a month, just for infants. Does it make sense for someone with a $3,000 to 4,000 a month salary to pay that much, for one child? Not when you consider the cost of working (taxes, transportation, clothing, etc.). Parents are forced to settle for more affordable programs.

I am not suggesting that cost is the only distinguishing factor between a high-quality and a substandard quality program. There are some great early childhood educators who have simply not reached master level or who do not have bachelors or master's degrees. What I *am* saying is that schools whose teachers and staff (all of them, not some) are appropriately trained in high-quality education practices, must charge higher tuitions.

Meanwhile, parents who can afford this high-quality education benefit in two ways. First, they're enrolling their youth in settings which provide the consistent opportunities and experiences for developing the skills of success. Second, the parents themselves are exposed to the best strategies for further supporting the quality home environments their youth need in order to reach their full potential. Administrators, teachers, and staff of high-quality early childhood education programs hold specialized teaching credentials and degrees which demonstrate their expertise in implementing the best practices for building extraOrdinary youth.

Unfortunately, far too many families in America don't receive these benefits and are on their own in learning how to get anything close to the same results. Additionally, parents, teachers, coaches, and other influencers of youth, have no training in early childhood education practices and have little or no information on the best strategies for helping young people build a positive self-image during their core developmental years. Most importantly, there hasn't been enough attention given to the impact which a positive self-image has on thinking, decisions, behaviors, and situational outcomes.

Many youngsters move into adolescence without the positive self-image they need to succeed. They're unequipped to successfully answer the questions: "Who am I?" and "What is my purpose?" To make matters worse, research which identifies the opportunities adolescents need to successfully move into adulthood has not yet been embraced the way high quality early childhood education has. Consequently, far too many young people move through adolescence without any opportunities to discover who they really are and what their purpose is. This is why young people and those who care for them face serious and unexpected challenges as the young person moves into adulthood. Young people need and deserve support. But they're not getting it because neither them nor the adults in their lives are aware of what they don't know.

All of this creates serious challenges for young people and their caregivers when it comes to self-image development. And since the quality of a young person's life is shaped by the quality of their thinking habits and by their self-image, it's vital that adult caregivers learn to answer these complex educational challenges.

Lastly, I'd like to add that it's not responsible to assume our children will learn these things through social interactions or at school—especially when *very* few of the children they interact with are getting this training. The school teachers and administrators have too many children under their care to make this a proper priority, even if they do have the specialized training. Leaving this development to chance is about as smart as putting a 15-year-old kid behind the wheel of a car and assuming they'll "figure it out."

We must be proactive about learning these strategies and applying them. The problem is, most parents simply don't know what they don't know. That's why, in the next chapter, we'll take a simple assessment and help you identify your own blind spots before we dive in.

Chapter 3: Make the Challenge—Assess What You Know

What do you mean we didn't come with a training manual?

1. Which parenting style yields the best overall outcome for a young person?

    A. Permissive-indulgent.

    B. Authoritarian.

    C. Authoritative.

    D. Avoidant.

    E. Balanced.

    F. A and B.

2. Which is the best way to raise self-reliant youth?

    A. Provide meaningful and specific acknowledgments, not flattery.

    B. Offer them opportunities to accomplish meaningful work.

    C. Use fair and consistent discipline.

    D. Nurture their needs, ideas, and requests.

3. Why is it critical for young people to form their identity and discover their purpose?

    A. Because without knowing who they are, they can't know what they stand for.

    B. Because if they don't know where they're going, they can't plan how to get there.

    C. Because identity drives their daily thinking, decisions, and behaviors and therefore shapes their entire life.

    D. All of the above.

4. What's the best way to support youth in building self-regulation and self-control?

    A. Don't discuss these topics, the skills will develop naturally.

    B. Help them find the words to identify their feelings and the needs attached to those feelings.

    C. Follow through on punishments.

    D. Allow natural consequences to occur.

5. What's the best thing for an adult to do when a young person makes a mistake?

    A. Use smart engagement.

    B. Help them learn from the mistake.

    C. Punish them.

    D. Use time-ins.

    E. A, B and D.

6. What do our thinking habits do?

    A. Direct our decisions.

    B. Affect our behaviors.

    C. Affect our quality of life.

    D. Either exacerbate or ameliorate our challenges.

    E. All of the above.

7. What shapes a young person's thinking habits?

    A. Their level of self-awareness.

    B. Their self-image.

    C. Their self-esteem.

    D. Their self-efficacy.

    E. All of the above.

8. What do you accomplish by creating a non-punitive environment for a young person to express themselves and to be heard?

   A. Discourage their misbehaviors.
   B. Cultivate their confidence.
   C. Indulge their demands.
   D. Build their communication skills.

9. What do adults accomplish when they connect with, acknowledge, and accept a young person's feelings without judgment?

   A. They help them develop coping strategies for dealing with challenges.
   B. They increase permissive and indulgent behaviors.
   C. They prove that adults have no boundaries.
   D. They spoil their young people.
   E. They open themselves up to manipulation.

10. What's a sure way to support youth, of any age, in developing a sense of mastery, autonomy, independence, and confidence?

    A. Use authoritarian parenting.
    B. Make sure their work is exceedingly challenging.
    C. Provide meaningful work—such as house chores.
    D. Make them master work that they're uninterested in,

11. What's one of the most powerful tools for helping young people assimilate new information?

    A. Repetition.
    B. Lecturing.
    C. Discussions.
    D. Modeling.

12. Which of the following strategies builds self-regulation, self-control, and confidence in young people?

    A. Flexible punishment.
    B. Logical and rigid consequences.
    C. Positive youth guidance.
    D. Punishment.
    E. Reinforcement.

13. Which is the best way to support young people in developing self-assertion skills, integrity, and perseverance?

    A. Lectures and discussions.
    B. Leading by example.
    C. Discouraging inappropriate peer relationships.
    D. Encouragement.
    E. Praising them when you catch them demonstrating these skills.

14. Which is an example of meaningful praise?

    A. "You look very pretty today."
    B. "Nancy, you look very pretty today."

C. "You worked hard to finish that project."

D. "Nancy, you worked hard to finish that project, but I can help you make it look a lot better!"

15. What does "meaningful connection" mean?

A. Providing undivided attention to another person's intellectual, creative, social, emotional and/or physical needs.

B. Texting while you're listening to someone.

C. Demonstrating, by behavior, that you think someone is important and significant.

D. A and C.

16. What is self-efficacy?

A. A person's belief in their ability to succeed in specific situations or to accomplish a task.

B. A person's perceptions of their own thoughts, personality, strengths, weaknesses, beliefs, motivations, and emotions.

C. A person's perceptions about what they look like on the outside, what their skills and abilities are and what their psychological states mean.

17. What is self-esteem?

A. A person's belief in their ability to succeed in specific situations or to accomplish a task.

B. A person's perception of their own thoughts, personality, strengths, weaknesses, beliefs, motivations, and emotions.

C. A person's perception about what they look like on the outside, what their skills and abilities are and what their psychological states mean.

D. A person's ability to experience themselves as capable of learning and making appropriate decisions towards reaching their goals.

E. A person's evaluation of their own thoughts, personality.

17. What is self-awareness?

A. A person's belief in their ability to succeed in specific situations or to accomplish a task.

B. A person's accurate understanding and evaluation of their abilities and preferences and of the impact their behavior has on others.

C. A person's ability to experience themselves as capable of learning and making appropriate decisions towards reaching their goals.

18. I'm knowledgeable about all of these issues and knew the answers immediately.

A. True.

B. False.

CORRECT ANSWERS

1. C
2. D
3. D
4. B
5. E
6. E
7. E
8. B
9. A
10. C
11. D
12. C
13. D
14. C
15. D
16. A
17. E
18. B

CHAPTER 4:
SELF-IMAGE AND THE PILLARS OF SELF-IMAGE

Merriam-Webster's Collegiate Dictionary (2016) defines self-image (self-concept or self-perception) as *how* we think about ourselves or the mental image we have of ourselves.

There are three pillars of self-image:

- Self-awareness
- Self-esteem
- Self-efficacy

I call them pillars because, depending on their strength or weakness, they can either support or weaken your overall self-image. Likewise, the strength of your overall self-image also shapes the development of each individual pillar.

Self-awareness is your capacity for introspection and the ability to recognize that you are separate from the environment and from other individuals. It's how you recognize and understand your own character, feelings, motives, and desires. There are two broad categories of self-awareness: internal self-awareness and external self-awareness. We'll get into these later. But it's important to understand that self-awareness is different than mere self-consciousness. Self-consciousness is your awareness of your environment, your body and your lifestyle, while self-awareness is the *recognition* of that awareness.

Self-esteem is your evaluation of your traits, characteristics, skills, etc. It's how you decide what these things are worth to *you* and to other people.

Self-efficacy refers to your individual belief in your capacity to perform a specific task or produce a specific outcome. It determines how confident you are in your ability to exert control over your own motivation, behavior, and social environment.

Pillar #1: Self-Awareness

Research expands the definition of self-awareness to include your mental image, mental construct, or mental concept of your personal traits or characteristics. This includes the images you have of your cognitive, creative, emotional, social, and physical skills and abilities, as well as your appearance, and your strengths and weaknesses (Hendrick & Weissman,

2014). Psychologists explain self-image as having two aspects: the *categorical self*—the sorting of one's self into categories, such as age, gender, skill, size or your roles within your family or workplace—and the *existential self*, which is your realization of being a separate entity from others with your own thoughts, beliefs, values, and preferences (Lewis, 1990; Montemayor & Eisen, 1977).

Lewis (1990) and Montemayor and Eisen (1977) suggest that there are four components to the **categorical self**.

- Your physical perception of yourself (e.g., "I'm short," "I have black hair," "I have green eyes").

- Your conception of your social roles (e.g., "I'm a teacher," I'm a mother," I'm a daughter," "I'm a basketball player," etc.).

- Your perspective of your personal traits (e.g., "I'm honest," "I'm intelligent," "I feel capable and worthy," "I can regulate my emotions well," etc.).

- Your statements describing the reason for your existence (e.g., "I'm a spiritual being" or "I'm a child of the universe," etc.).

The **Existential Self** is the most basic part of the self-image. It's the seat of our self-awareness. According to Lewis and Brooks-Gun (1979), the existential self, or self-awareness, emerges when a baby is just twelve months old and becomes more developed at eighteen months.

As youth develop, so does their self-awareness. They discover that their thoughts, personalities, strengths, weaknesses, beliefs, motivations, and emotions are separate from those of others. A young person's self-awareness continues to develop as skills, abilities, and preferences take shape. As they compare themselves to others and listen to the many messages they receive from their primary caregivers, young people become more aware of their strengths and their weaknesses. Furnham (2011) describes self-awareness as a person's accurate understanding and evaluation of his or her own abilities and preferences and the impact which one's behavior has on others. He also says that self-awareness allows individuals to reach their goals because it helps them understand where they are, so that they can plan how to get where they want to go.

META-SELF-AWARENESS

the "supervisor" of your self-awareness. Alain Morin (2006) defines "meta-self-awareness" as being "aware that one is self-aware." You might call it the ability to examine your own internal states, as opposed to simply experiencing and identifying them. David R. Vago and David A. Silbersweig (2012) describe meta-self-awareness as the key to exercising self-regulation. For example, a self-aware person could say,

"I'm angry," but in a state of meta-self-awareness the same person could state, "I'm aware that I'm in a state of anger" or "I'm analyzing my emotional state of anger." Such a person can regulate and control their emotions, while a person without meta-self-awareness is more likely to be controlled by their emotions.

META-SELF-AWARENESS SKILL

Self-regulation—a state of awareness that empowers you to explore your thoughts and emotions and choose self-control before taking action. **This is the most important skill for setting and achieving your goals.**

Self-regulation is also essential to emotional well-being. We call it a "meta-self-awareness skill" because it allows us to examine our emotions and thoughts as they occur—even during challenging situations. This makes it the master key to self-control. Stosny (2011) identifies two "prongs" to self-regulation:

- Emotional self-regulation.
- Behavioral self-regulation.

Emotional self-regulation is the ability to calm yourself down when you're upset and to examine your own thoughts and moods. Behavioral self-regulation is the ability to use self-control to regulate your own behaviors. Therefore, achieving a balance between emotional and behavioral self-regulation is the key to acting in a way that's consistent with your personal values. For example, think of a person who has a lot of will power when it comes to achieving tasks, completing projects on time or sticking with a workout routine. But at other times, this person might have a hard time controlling their emotions. This is an example of someone with strong behavioral self-regulation, but poor emotional self-regulation.

By using meta-self-awareness to develop a healthy balance between emotional and behavioral self-regulation, you become empowered to live by your values instead of being controlled by your moods and by circumstances. This is how you avoid guilt, shame, and anxiety—all of which are the result of making decisions that are inconsistent with your personal values. This works even when things don't go your way. For example, a student may do poorly in math, and with *self-awareness* that student will likely perceive that he's simply "bad at math." But meta-self-awareness gives him the self-regulating skills to step in and change something, instead of feeling helpless. For example, students with strong self-regulation will ask for help rather than give up (Vago & Silbersweig, 2012; Zimmerman, 2002). This would be an example of the student using self-regulation to manage his own behaviors, and intercede on his own behalf. But the student can also know that if he cheats on the exam, instead of asking for help, it could damage his well-being because he believes that cheating is wrong. This is an example of self-regulation helping the student to live by his own values. Without these skills, the student is at the mercy of his emotions and of the circumstances which created them. This is why it is so important for caregivers to provide young people with opportunities to choose their own values and to discover how to live by those values.

BENEFITS OF SELF-AWARENESS AND META SELF-AWARENESS

Self-Regulation is the key to self-control. Without it, you will be controlled by your moods, by circumstances and/or by other people's opinions. Think of self-regulation as an internal thinking process and self-control as the power to "control" your external behaviors. Self-awareness coach Guy Farmer (n.d.) compiled the following list which reflects his research on the subject:

- The ability to act consciously instead of reacting to people and events (self-regulation)

- The ability to genuinely love yourself

- Being authentically happy rather than pretending you are

- Greater depth of experience and enjoyment of life

- The ability to redirect your negative thoughts and emphasize positive ones

- Behaving positively instead of creating additional obstacles

- Enjoying positive interpersonal relationships

- Being the real you

- Living courageously and without limits

- The ability to make your dreams come true

Dr. Scott Williams (n.d.) of Wright State University suggests that self-awareness and meta-self-awareness skills allow individuals to motivate themselves and others, to manage stress, and to make intuitive decisions.

Tjan (2015) writes, in the *Harvard Business Review*, "You can't be a good leader without *self-awareness*." Sara Canaday (2013) reports that self-awareness and meta-self-awareness skills are also the cornerstone of emotional intelligence. Such skills empower you to self-regulate by tuning in to your thoughts and feelings and assessing the best actions before you act.

In summary, self-image is how you experience and manage your own moods, beliefs, skills, roles and behaviors. The research discussed above defines and describes the relationship between self-awareness, meta-self-awareness skills, and self-image—and how they can work together to make a person happier and more resourceful.

PILLAR #2: SELF-ESTEEM

There are many misconceptions about what self-esteem is and what it does for an individual. Because of these misconceptions, many people believe that kids need praise whether they have earned it or not. We allow children to automatically move up a grade in school despite failing every class.

These ridiculous decisions are based on the misconception of self-esteem. We don't want to "hurt their self-esteem" by suggesting they are not good enough or equal to the other children.

I might suck at using my social skills, but I am pure genius at this gaming stuff!

We assume this would cause irreversible damage to them. The problem with these thoughts of course is that they are delusional. Children who fail all of their classes and get to move up a grade know the truth! They know they are different from the children who earned passing grades. They know they haven't advanced by their own merits. Passing them anyway causes more harm in the long run because it stops them from developing a sense of accomplishment and might even make them feel entitled to things they didn't earn.

Here is what we know about self-esteem: high self-esteem does not guarantee a healthy self-image and can even prove detrimental to your well-being. Case in point, scales which measure high esteem have shown that many people who are incarcerated or have chosen other anti-social behaviors actually score well on these scales, because they perceive themselves as smarter than others. This means that positive self-esteem alone is *not* enough for living a successful, significant, meaningful, productive, joyful life. It must be joined with the experiences needed to build self-regulation, self-control, and strong senses of self-efficacy. More importantly, by itself positive self-esteem doesn't necessarily lead to a positive self-image!

In Healthy Lifestyle Adult Health, the Mayo Clinic Staff stated that, "self-esteem begins to form in early childhood. Factors that can influence self-esteem include:

- Your thoughts and perceptions
- How other people react to you
- Experiences at home, school, work and in the community
- Illness, disability or injury
- Age
- Role and status in society
- Media messages

Self-esteem is based on one's evaluation or assessment of their self-image (existential and categorical self). Coopersmith (1990) defined self-esteem as personal judgment of worthiness that is expressed by attitudes individuals hold toward their self-image (e.g., traits, characteristics, and society roles). According to Zeigler-Hill (2013) self-esteem always involves self-assessment *and* self-evaluation of our personal traits. Self-esteem is a concept that refers to a person's overall evaluation of themselves and the appraisal of their own worth (Cherry, 2017). In "The Pillars of the Self-Concept: self-esteem and self-efficacy," Frank, 2011, p. 1, writes:

> **"We all have a sense of self. Whether that sense of self is positive or negative is based upon our experiences in life and our perceptions and assessments of ourselves."**

While this is true, our perceptions of ourselves can also be distorted by our experiences.

To clarify the difference, and the relationship, between self-image and self-esteem, think of someone you know who considers themselves a "talkative" person. That's their self-image identifying one of their traits. But their self-esteem will determine their attitude towards the talkative trait itself. Do they value being talkative? Do they see it as beneficial? Or do they consider it a nuisance and worry that it might drive people away or cause other types of problems? In other words, do they *esteem* their talkative behavior as something positive or negative? This would be an example of the person's self-esteem at work in evaluating a single character trait.

Our overall self-esteem, however, is based on the sum total of positive *and* negative evaluations of our existential and categorical traits. So the more favorable assessment we have of these traits, the more positive our overall self-esteem will be.

The opposite is also true. Assessing many of our traits and characteristics unfavorably contributes to an overall negative self-esteem.

Leary and Baumeister (2004) proposed that self-esteem is the extent to which we like, accept, or approve of ourselves, or the overall value we place on ourselves. Positive self-esteem is defined as a person's ability to experience oneself as being capable of learning, making appropriate choices and decisions to reach goals, and having the competence to cope with life's basic challenges. Nathaniel Branden (1995) suggests that favorable opinions of one's traits provides a basic belief that the self is worthy of happiness, success, and achievement.

People with negative self-esteem typically don't perceive themselves as competent. This kind of thinking disrupts their motivation to manage their environmental circumstances. Consequently, people with negative self-esteem are shown to have a harder time managing challenging situations. They also lack confidence in their ability to successfully deal with circumstances which lie outside their known skill set (Cohen, n.d.).

People with negative self-esteem are more troubled by failure and tend to identify most situations as negative. Their fear of failure and negative thinking results in a helpless mind-set. Youth with negative self-esteem may come to rely on counterproductive coping strategies. For example, they might resort to bullying, quitting, cheating, avoidance, etc. They'll also give in to peer pressure, rather than standing up for their own beliefs. At school, they'll give up easily when challenged and they'll avoid trying new things for fear of failure (McLeod, 2012).

BENEFITS OF POSITIVE SELF-ESTEEM

There are many benefits of positive self-esteem. Gathered below are articles presented from various professional sources which describe these benefits. You'll notice similarities among the lists of benefits. The following statement was published in the article, "Self-esteem check: Too low or just right?" in Healthy Lifestyle, self-esteem and the benefits of self-esteem are discussed.

> **"When you value yourself and have good self-esteem, you feel secure and worthwhile. You have generally positive relationships with others and feel confident about your abilities. You're also open to learning and feedback, which can help you acquire and master new skills."**

Those with healthy self-esteem are:

- Assertive in expressing needs and opinions
- Confident in their ability to make decisions

- Able to form secure and honest relationships—and less likely to stay in unhealthy ones

- Realistic in their expectations and less likely to be over-critical of themselves and others

- More resilient and better able to weather stress and setbacks

In his course "How to be More Confident" Fonvielle (n.d.) describes benefits of positive self-esteem as:

- More happiness and enjoyment in life: When you see lots of positive value in yourself, you're naturally happier with yourself and your life.

- A more worthwhile and meaningful life: By extension, the more value you see in yourself and your life, the more life feels worthwhile, meaningful, and worth living.

- A healthier and better lifestyle: If you see lots of positive value in yourself, you'll naturally take care of yourself better, and you'll naturally seek ways to improve yourself and your well-being.

- More confidence: When you see lots of value in yourself and your capabilities, you naturally think that other people will like and value you, and you naturally think you'll achieve things you want to achieve. In this way, positive self-esteem leads to positive self-confidence, so this is how to be confident and have positive self-esteem naturally and easily.

- More success in life: The more confident you are, due to positive self-esteem, the more likely you are to try to achieve things you want to achieve. This naturally makes you more successful.

- More peace of mind: When you see lots of positive value in yourself and your capabilities, it's naturally easy for you to think that you can accept and handle different challenges in life. This naturally makes you a more calm, relaxed, and peaceful person and frees you from a great deal of stress and anxiety.

- More enjoyable social interactions: When you think positively about yourself and your capabilities, you're happier and more confident around other people, and this naturally leads to more enjoyable social interactions.

In summary, self-esteem is your evaluation and judgment of your own personal traits and/or characteristics. It determines your attitude about your overall worthiness as a person. It is one of the pillars of self-image. Positive self-esteem builds support for a positive self-image. Negative self-esteem fails to support a positive self-image. The research discussed above defines and describes how this happens.

There is also an intricate relationship between self-image, self-esteem, and self-efficacy (Frank, 2011), which we'll talk about right now.

Pillar #3: Self-Efficacy (The 'Locus of Control')

According to psychologist Albert Bandura (2012), *self-efficacy* is your belief in your own ability to succeed in specific situations or to accomplish a task. *Self-efficacy* plays a major role in how you approach goals, tasks, and challenges.

Bandura identified self-efficacy as one's internal *locus of control*. A person with an external locus of control does not believe they can influence events and outcomes. They tend to blame external factors for their lack of ability to do so. In other words, they give their power away to external things. This is a self-fulfilling prophecy because, while it comes from a lack in their sense of self-empowerment, it also makes them feel more powerless. On the other hand, people with an *internal* locus of control believe they can influence events and outcomes. This is because such people believe in their own abilities to accomplish whatever tasks are necessary to get what they want. This makes an internal locus of control an empowering mechanism for those who possess it.

Bandura referred to people with a strong internal locus of control as having strong self-efficacy. According to Bandura, a person's attitudes, abilities, and intellectual skills comprise what is known as the "self-system." This system plays a major role in how we perceive situations and how we behave in response to them. This makes self-efficacy an essential part of our self-system.

Self-Efficacy is one of the pillars of self-image because it determines your belief in your ability to accomplish a specific goal or task. You can believe yourself to be competent in accomplishing certain tasks, and yet believe you're incompetent in accomplishing others. That said, when you have a strong sense of self-efficacy, you will maintain, in general, a basic belief that you're capable of accomplishing most of the goals you set and tasks you take on (Frank, 2011). Miriam Akhtar (2017) agrees with this, and also suggests that self-efficacy is a form of confidence.

In summary, self-efficacy plays a pivotal role in how you live your life. Gandhi (n.d.) said, "Your beliefs become your thoughts. Your thoughts become your words. Your words become your actions. Your actions become your habits. Your habits become your values. Your values become your destiny."

BENEFITS OF A STRONG SENSE OF SELF-EFFICACY

- Those with a strong self-efficacy can develop successful action plans to accomplish their goals. They make this look easy.

- They enjoy deeper interest in the activities they participate in.

- They enjoy a stronger sense of commitment to their interests and activities.

- They recover well from unexpected setbacks and frustrations.

- They see problems as "challenges" and as something to be overcome and/or mastered.

- They spend little or no time complaining about problems, and more time troubleshooting and coming up with solutions.

Author's Summary and Perspective

In this chapter, we've discussed the complex nature of "self-image." We've defined self-image as the perception or concept a person has of who he or she is. We've talked about meta-self-awareness and its role in developing self-regulation, self-esteem, and a strong sense of self-efficacy. We've also begun to discuss the impact self-image has on thinking, behavior, and outcomes. We've talked about how our belief in who we are and what we are capable of affects how we approach goals, tasks, and challenges. In the next Chapter, we'll talk about how to empower young people to develop these essential skills and build an extraOrdinary self-image.

Chapter 5:
Meaningful Connections

As a college professor, I taught aspiring teachers to build curriculum for teaching intellectual skills *in a way that* promotes, supports, and shapes the development of positive self-image in their students. I taught future teachers to do this by making what I call "meaningful connections" with young people. I emphasized such connections as a means of turning students' missteps, mistakes, and even their inappropriate behaviors into learning opportunities. This was my work as an early childhood educator and psychology professor.

At the heart of a meaningful connection is the adult's desire to:

- Understand, respect, and be sensitive to a young person's developmental, intellectual, creative, emotional, social, physical abilities, skills, and yes, their behaviors.

- Encourage further positive development of the *whole person.*

- Elicit the young person's thinking, ideas, possible solutions to problems, and thinking outside of the box, etc.

- Deliver powerful messages to young people about what we think of them.

- Tell kids that we are on their side, that we love and care about them unconditionally and that we are there to support them despite their mistakes.

Meaningful connections are the most powerful way to say to a young person, "you matter, you are important, you are worthy of my time and patience!" These are the messages which support a positive self-image.

Making meaningful connections does not mean withholding consequences for disrespectful, bad, rude, or obnoxious behaviors. It does not mean adults should become doormats or give young people the impression that they aren't accountable for their actions. Learning how to make meaningful connections takes time, effort and, for most of us, special training.

Unfortunately, the topic and training, to my knowledge, takes place in early childhood education classes like those I taught. It's not part of our mainstream education agenda. Very little is said about the importance of making meaningful connections with adolescents, age 11 to 21 years—let alone how to do it. This means we have parents, guardians, school teachers, staff, and administrators, coaches, mentors, tutors, volunteers, and spiritual leaders working with youth everyday who have no idea how to use meaningful connections, when to use them, or even how significant they are.

THE NEED FOR MEANINGFUL CONNECTIONS

Humans are biologically driven to make meaningful connections. Call it Mother Nature's way of ensuring our survival. Our creativity is nurtured by connections which support and encourage our natural talents and interests. Our creative self is the source of our joy and of the service we give to others. Meaningful connections also satisfy our social and emotional needs, making them essential for our safety, health, well-being, and survival.

As adults, we need to understand that freedom-seeking adolescents need connections with us just as much as they did when they were infants. Unfortunately, many adolescents are at high risk for NOT experiencing these connections. This is because adults focus mainly on a young person's physical and educational needs, and most adolescents can take care of these on their own. For example, when teachers assign homework or announce upcoming exams, they expect adolescents to prepare accordingly. Parents remind adolescents to do their homework and they assume that they're preparing for exams. And, although most adolescents have no formal training in accomplishing these tasks, we assume they'll "figure it out." But, when it comes to supporting adolescents in meeting their creative, social, and emotional needs, most of us have limited time to do it. Most importantly, very few of us have any training at all in this area.

Another problem is that when our kids are acting inappropriately, during adolescence, we tend to scold them or ask them questions such as, "What the heck were you thinking?" or "What the heck is wrong with you?" How can we expect young people to feel good about themselves if the majority of messages they hear from us are only about controlling their behaviors? At some point they need us to engage with them and encourage them to stop, think, and then make a decision that leads to getting their needs met with appropriate actions. When kids are given these opportunities they build healthy thinking habits, they have more success navigating their daily lives, they feel really good about themselves, they trust themselves, and they trust us to be on their side.

Of course the opposite is also true. When kids are not given opportunities and encouraged to stop and think before they make decisions how can they learn to do so? If all we do is scold them, put them down, and punish them when they behave inappropriately or make mistakes then there is a strong chance that they'll come to believe that they are losers or that something is wrong with them. Building meaningful connections doesn't mean tolerating bad behavior. It doesn't mean we allow our children to disrespect us. There are specific strategies used in meaningful connections so that adults do not walk away feeling as though they are turning themselves into doormats.

ADOLESCENTS' BIG NEED FOR MEANINGFUL CONNECTIONS

> **"They can be forgetful, lazy, rude, hurt, act like they don't care, and we know that one wrong decision can change everything—which is why meaningful connections during this time is critical!" -Dr. Kim**

> **"They may pretend that they don't need you, don't believe it, they need you as much during adolescence as during infancy." -Dr. Kim**

Adolescence (ages 11 to 21) is the time when young people become adults. Preteens, teens, and young adults spend this time exploring, discovering, and deciding what their personal values and beliefs will be. They experiment with various behaviors and they try on different identities. These experiments help them discover what feels good and what doesn't so they can develop a solid identity and live by their values in all areas of their lives. This is the process of forming an identity, and adolescence, according to all of the research is the time period in which it begins.

Adolescence is also the time for discovering personal talents and interests. These discoveries help young people decide what they want to do with their future. It helps them draw a "road map" of the goals and actions which will lead them to their dreams. Everyone needs this, and meaningful connections with loving and caring adults will help a young person to find it so they can live a deeply purposeful and fulfilling life.

I think we'll agree that a productive, meaningful, and joyful life is a good life. But to have these things, you must know who you are and what really matters to you. Most importantly, you need a purpose which reflects your values and which allows you to make the most of your natural talents and interests. This is how you find significance as a member of society. To accomplish this, you must know the answer to three questions:

- Who am I?
- What is my purpose?
- Am I a significant member of society?

Meaningful connections allow adults to deliver messages which shape an adolescent's self-perspective and help them answer these questions. Such messages cause a young person to think things like: "I'm valuable," "I'm important," "I matter" or "I'm a priority." This is how adults provide meaningful connections with adolescents and help them to build a positive self-image. If you forget everything else you've read in this book, please remember this. I'll say it again—building meaningful connections means helping a young person develop a positive self-image. Remember, a young person's self-image determines the life they end up living. A truly positive self-image will make them absolutely certain of who they are and what matters to them, even when nothing else in their life makes sense.

The human need to make meaningful connections and to "feel" significant is so powerful that if it goes unmet for long periods of time, we will *choose* unhealthy behaviors as a substitute for meeting them. For example, some people try to meet these needs through excessive use of technology (e.g., video games, cell phones, social media). These may seem like harmless behaviors. But the technology companies who design our "toys" have access to billions of dollars in research on how to make their products addictive by eliciting dopamine releases in our brains. You might even say that more time and money goes into making technology addictive than goes into developing addictive drugs. On the other hand, some people choose numbing behaviors like drugs (legal or illegal) or alcohol. They use these because they need to "not feel" the pain which comes from a lack of connection. Other young people self-medicate using their emotions. They become hostile, aggressive, angry, and/or indulge in violent behavior, including gun violence, just so they can "feel something." The common thread in all of these behaviors is that they *remove individuals from the real world* where meaningful connections happen.

Bottom line, adults who interact with youth can make a significant impact on the young person's creative, social, and emotional wellness by helping the young person meet their needs within the context of real life. All it takes is intentionally choosing these meaningful interactions—and all that takes is awareness, effort and persistence.

Let's start by exploring some of the obstacles that keep these meaningful connections from happening.

IMPEDIMENTS TO MEANINGFUL CONNECTIONS

Young people who live with stress and/or trauma—whether due to family dysfunction, social challenges, or insecure attachment—are at high risk for not getting the meaningful connections they need. These kids are also unlikely to get their creative, emotional, and/or social needs met consistently. Keep in mind that kids like Abbey do not necessarily present themselves as "at risk." They do well in school and in a variety of social settings. This is why so many adults do not perceive them as kids who need meaningful connections. These are the *invisible kids* we talked about in Chapter One. Adults can completely misread which kids need help and which kids are getting what they need. In fact, given that almost half of the kids living in the US are experiencing at least one stressful and traumatic situation during the developmental years, it is more likely than not that one or more young person you work with will benefit from having meaningful connections outside of their homes. Let's consider some of the situations young people endure which make them less likely to get the meaningful connections they need.

FAMILY DYSFUNCTION

Family dysfunction can result from extreme poverty, homelessness, parents' divorce, forms of child abuse, parental mental or physical illness, death of a parent, incarceration of a parent, drug and/or alcohol abuse in the home, etc. Other factors might include poor child health, income instability, or anything else that causes extreme stress on the family. These situations place tremendous stress on families and are a major disruptor of meaningful connections in the home.

SOCIAL CHALLENGES

The Minority Stress Model describes social issues which cause stress and trauma for young people. It defines "Minority Stress" as something which results from a stressful or hostile social environment. This would be any environment that exposes a young person to stigma, prejudice, rejection, and/or discrimination. These stressors can be directed at the young person because of their race, gender identity, sexuality, religion, and/or national origin. A young person exposed to such trauma may hide, conceal, or pretend in order to avoid the rejection, ridicule or other negative treatment from others. These are unhealthy coping mechanisms which further compound the young person's stress and discomfort (Meyer, 2003). Hiding concealing and pretending makes it less likely for these young people to reach out and make the meaning-ful connections they really need. Imagine if all adults who interact with youth were prone to make meaningful connec-tions, these kids despite their inability to reach out, would surely benefit from this tactic.

INSECURE ATTACHMENT

At the very foundation of insecure attachment is the lack of a primary caretaker to make any meaningful connection with their infant. John Bowlby's attachment theory explains vari-ous types of bonds formed between infants and their caregiv-ers. There are two types of attachment: 1) secure attachment and 2) insecure attachment. Collective research indicates that secure attachment influences the development of pos-itive self-image, whereas insecure attachment influences the development of negative self-image.

Insecurely attached youth present different types of behav-iors, and these behaviors are described as anxious-insecure, avoidant-insecure, or ambivalent-insecure (Holmes, 2014). For example, Dozier and Lee (1995) found that people with either avoidant or ambivalent insecure attachment have a distorted self-image due to their early interactions with care-givers. Kaslow, Adamson, and Collins (2000) report that an individual's self-image and their perceptions of others is sig-nificantly affected by their early infant-parent attachment style.

Gamble and Roberts (2005) found that insecure attachment can lead to negative self-esteem. Kuiper and Olinger (1986) and Roberts et. al. (1996) found that insecure attachment was associated with dysfunctional attitudes, which also produce negative self-esteem. Why do attachment patterns have such an impact on young people's self-image? Because young people make decisions about themselves, others, and the world based on their early relationships. They build internal mental representations (working models) of themselves, and others based on the quality of these relationships. These models become a young person's beliefs about who they are, how the world works, how they fit into the world, and what they must do to be accepted in it.

Securely attached youth develop mental structures which result in them feeling worthy of care, love, and positive attention. They also form positive self-images as a result of these secure attachments. However, insecurely attached youth develop working models which result in them seeing themselves as unworthy and unlovable—leading to a negative self-image (Adler, 1956).

Some psychologists have proposed that parents who provide quality care (emotionally appropriate responses—*Meaningful Connections*) for youth send messages of acceptance, support, and the encouragement to explore, despite mistakes or failures. Securely attached infants and youth learn that if they make a mistake, a trusted caregiver will respond appropriately. Because of this, securely attached youth persist in learning tasks until they become competent in them. And when they become competent in skills that are meaningful to them, they build positive self-esteem (Buri et al., 1988) and a strong sense of self-efficacy (Bandura, 1977).

Insecurely attached infants grow up in an environment where no meaningful connections are present to help them develop healthy intellectual, emotional, and social skills. This can even retard their physical development. They live in constant fear because they do not trust that their needs will be met. Since our early relationships become models for all future relationships, insecure attachment has a negative impact on a child's thinking and behaviors and this impact sends ripples through the child's entire life.

There are stark differences when comparing brain development, thinking habits, and behaviors of securely and insecurely attached youth. Insecurely attached youth have challenges in almost every environment. Whether in foster care, schools, or participating in extracurricular activities, they have poor self-regulation, little or no self-control, and low self-confidence.

I was shocked to discover that almost 50% of youth living in the US are insecurely attached. These statistics prove that anyone working with youth are dealing with the challenges related to insecure attachment. That's why I dedicated an entire chapter in the bonus section of this book to explain the thinking and behaviors typical to insecurely attached kids. Because of the prevalence of insecure attachment and the challenges insecurely attached youth face, it would be beneficial for adults who work with youth to be familiar with their behaviors and ways to help these kids. This starts with understanding exactly how self-image impacts a young person's habitual thinking and decision making.

Chapter 6:
Thinking Habits and Self-Image

Thinking

Thinking is defined as "the process of considering or reasoning about something; the action of using one's mind to produce thoughts, opinions, judgments and decisions" (*Merriam-Webster's Collegiate Dictionary*, 2016; Oxford Dictionary, 2018). Whatever you think about thinking, you can't do anything without it, so you'd better do it well. Psychology offers theories and research which allow us to describe, predict, and understand relationships between the variables of thinking, motivation, attitudes, and observable behaviors. Complex relationships exist between these variables (Wood & Fabrigar, 2015). The link between our beliefs, our thinking habits, and our behaviors cannot be denied. Specifically, our thinking habits influence our decisions, our decisions influence our behaviors, and our behaviors impact daily situations. This impact can be harmless, harmful, or beneficial in many ways.

THINKING HABITS AND SELF-IMAGE

Our thinking, whether negative, positive, or indifferent, does not come from a land far, far away, nor does it stream into our brains from outer space. Our thinking comes from our own minds and is shaped by our self-image.

Consider the impact that your thinking has on every situation in your life! It directs your decisions and behaviors, and therefore shapes the consequences you end up living with. So, what directs your thinking? Your basic mental concepts about yourself, including:

- **Self-Image:** your perception of your own physical appearance, and of your intellectual, creative, emotional, social, and physical abilities.

- **Self-Awareness:** being aware of our own character and personality traits, of our behaviors and of the needs which drive those behaviors.

- **Self-Esteem:** your personal evaluation of the self-awareness traits listed above—this is how you determine what these traits are worth to you and why they matter.

- **Self-Efficacy:** your beliefs about your own capacity to execute behaviors which will help you achieve your goals and duties.

These mental concepts shape your thinking and your behavior, and therefore they determine what kind of life you'll end up living and, most importantly, how satisfied you are with that life.

THINKING HABITS: FIXED MINDSET VS GROWTH MINDSET

A habit is defined as "a settled tendency or usual manner of behavior," or "an acquired mode of behavior that has become nearly or completely involuntary" (Merriam-Webster's Collegiate Dictionary, 2018). As you know, habits are hard to break, especially thinking habits. A thinking habit is any default pattern we use to decide

101

what we will do in a situation or type of situation. Carol Dweck (2017) stressed that paying attention to the way you think about your abilities (self-image, self-esteem) can be a game-changer. She describes two default mind-sets—fixed and open—both of which develop directly from one's self-perception. Those who think using a fixed mind-set believe their basic abilities—their intelligence and their talents—are fixed traits. Those who think using a growth mind-set understand that their talents and abilities can be developed and improved through persistence, effort, and good instruction.

Influence of Mindset

An adult's praise of a young person plays a major role in the kind of mindset the young person develops. Dweck's research reveals two ways to praise someone and describes how an adult's praise directly affects a young person's beliefs about themselves.

Type one, called "person praise," focuses on the person's characteristics, intelligence, and creativity. Here are two examples of *person praise*:

- "Good job, you must be smart!"
- "Look how good you are in English you earned an A."

Person praise leads young people to believe that their success is based on their intelligence and talents. Young people who receive this kind of praise come to believe that their traits, intelligence, and creativity are fixed. If they're challenged, if they don't do well on a task, or if they fail, they believe it's because they're not smart enough or not creative enough.

Type two, called "process praise," produces the opposite outcome. Here are two examples of *process praise*:

- "Great job! You must have worked really hard!"
- "You really studied for your English test and your effort shows."

Because processes can be improved (e.g., you can work harder, or study harder) young people who receive *process praise* develop a mindset that opens them up to possibilities for improving their skills and overcoming challenges. We'll talk more about how to use *process praise* in *The Positive Youth Guidance System* (see Chapter 9). For now, the important thing to understand is that *person praise* limits growth, while *process praise* leaves room for it.

As stated earlier, our thinking does not stream into our mind from a land far, far away. It comes *from* our mind, where it is formulated. We choose what we think about. More importantly, we choose *how* to think about it. *How* we think about information is significantly impacted by *how* we think about ourselves, and by *how* we think about our abilities. For example, imagine the impact thoughts as simple as these could have on any person's life:

- "I'm intelligent, and therefore I can."

- "I'm capable, and therefore I will."
- "I'm worthy, and therefore I deserve."

I think you'll agree that you're more likely to act on your best intentions when you're convinced that you will succeed. This is how the thinking in the examples above assures that you'll make the most of your best intentions. Without it, even the best intentions never get acted on and never have the chance to make an impact in your life or in the world.

THINKING TOWARD AN EXTRAORDINARY LIFE

We all want our young people to live extraOrdinary lives. An extraOrdinary life looks different for different people. Since humans are unique, definitions of an "extraOrdinary life" are probably as vast as the number of humans on the planet. We all have different values, beliefs, talents, and interests that shape our individual dreams and goals. So I would argue that an extraOrdinary life can only be lived by those who know themselves, who love themselves, and who are true to themselves. Without a positive self-image, we cannot know who we are, or love who we are, or be true to who we are. We cannot persist when challenges arise and we cannot intervene on our own behalf.

CAREGIVERS AS GATEKEEPERS OF YOUTH'S DREAMS AND GOALS

What happens between the time children dream and the time when they realize their dreams will never come true?

All young people dream about who they will become and what they will do when they grow up. But adults play a significant role in whether these young people will ever achieve their dreams. Adults who parent or work with youth are in charge of preparing young people to live independent lives and to develop the thinking habits and skills that will help them reach their goals, realize their dreams, and live the lives they want to live.

Considering this, it's important that *all* of us are equipped with the tools for becoming responsible, encouraging gatekeepers. And the foundation of this is building meaningful connections with young people using the strategies in the *Positive Youth Guidance System.*

Author's Summary and Perspective

In this chapter, we've discussed the interplay between self-image, thinking, and behaviors. We've talked about how positive self-image brings about confident thinking, allowing you to act on your own behalf and in alignment with your personal value system. We've talked about how a negative self-image causes you to doubt your capabilities and ideas. A negative self-image sabotages your ability to act effectively (e.g., feelings of helplessness based on the belief that "life happens to me and I have no control"). But a positive self-image enhances your belief that you can act effectively. Most importantly, we've talked about how a young persons' self-image significantly affects their thinking, behavior, and outcomes.

Since young people carry their self-image into adulthood, it's crucial that you have the tools to understand how a young person's self-image is formed. The following diagrams will help:

- Diagram 6.1 Impact of Thinking on Behavior
- Diagram 6.2 Three Pillars of Self-Image

DIAGRAM 6.1 IMPACT OF THINKING ON BEHAVIOR

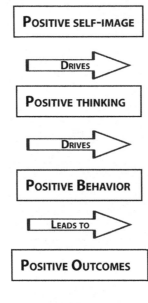

I REACH MY GOALS!

DIAGRAM 6.2 THREE PILLARS OF SELF-IMAGE

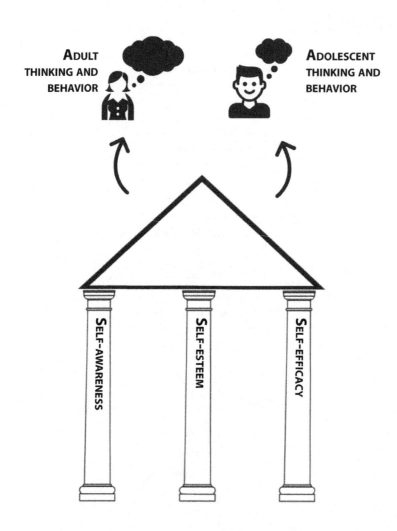

Chapter 7: The Relationship among Development, Learning, and Caretaking

Given the significant impact that a young person's self-image has on their thinking, behavior, and life, it is worth exploring how the self-image is developed within the context of adult to youth relationships. In this section, we'll explore how caregivers influence the development of a young person's self-image through their influence on the three pillars of self-image.

SETTLING THE 'NATURE VS NURTURE' DEBATE

A young person's development is shaped by both biology, genetics (nature), the environment (nurture), and by the interaction between the two. Our biology makes us human, and therefore we develop the traits and characteristics of humans. Our genetics also direct the unique ways our human traits will be expressed or passed on to our offspring. Biological and genetic effects of development occur at the moment of conception, and these cannot be undone. The only exception is when advanced surgery can be used to correct a correctable abnormality.

The environment, however, can be altered tremendously from the moment of conception until the end of a person's life. Biology and genetics work to effect development from within the person. Scientists refer to this as nature's influence on human development. On the other hand, the environment is everything that influences a person from the outside. This is what scientists call "nurture." The research shows that primary caregivers have the biggest impact of a young person's overall development—including self-image development. *Youth learn from their primary caregivers* and *learning* impacts all aspects of development!

Learning and development are inseparable. In fact, most human development happens through the learning process. We learn by repeatedly experiencing the same thing. Some experiences are negative and others are positive. Nevertheless, we learn from the information that is repeatedly presented to us and we learn, in a variety of ways, from our primary caregivers.

While it is true that humans are genetically predisposed to specific talents, they must have the opportunity to develop and express these talents. What matters most, however, is the way a young person views themselves, others, their community, the world, and their purpose in the world. A young person who understands these things clearly is more likely to live a meaningful, significant, joyful life. And who helps a young person understand these things for themselves? In a perfect world, their parents, teachers, family, coaches, tutors, older siblings, employers, spiritual leaders, and adults who volunteer in their extracurricular activities would help them do so. Here's how that would happen:

- Adults would model appropriate behaviors (self-regulation, self-control, positive self-image, self-love, self-care, self-respect, respect of others, open-mindedness, mindfulness).

- Adults would provide learning opportunities and experiences to foster growth and development.

- Adults would provide encouragement to persist when challenges arise.

- Adults would provide emotional support.

- Adults would use an authoritative caretaking style.

- Adults would use positive youth guidance.

- Adults would use age and ability appropriate communication.

Adults can make this happen by using specific interaction strategies with youth such as those found in the Positive Youth Guidance System (Chapter 9 of this book).

This list may look intimidating at first. But remember, the purpose of this book is to turn these practices into habits. New habits always seem impossible when you first start trying to learn them. But after some practice, they'll become less daunting. If you stick with these strategies until they become second nature, you'll eventually wonder how they ever could have been hard. Most things in life are like this. Just think about all the things you struggled to learn, but you now do almost instinctively. If you follow the simple strategies in the *Positive Youth Guidance System*, building meaningful connections will work out the same way.

THREE CAREGIVING STYLES THAT IMPEDE HEALTHY DEVELOPMENT

There are four caregiving styles. Most caregivers use all four, but tend to favor one as their primary, and this primary style has the most significant effect on the overall development of the young people they care for. Authoritative caretaking, is discussed in the *Positive Youth Guidance System* (see chapter 9), is considered the ideal style because it yields the best outcomes for young people. Caregivers who primarily use *Authoritarian, Permissive-Indulgent, and Avoidant-Uninvolved provide far fewer opportunities for young people to develop the skills that are needed for healthy development. These* three styles are discussed below to make it easier for caregivers to identify their use of them and self-correct to the authoritative style.

STYLE 1: AUTHORITARIAN

Motto: *"Youth should be seen and not heard!"*

CHARACTERISTICS OF AUTHORITARIAN CAREGIVERS

Authoritarian caregivers exhibit the following behaviors:

- Cold, rigid and inflexible.

- Overly strict.

- Expects unquestioning obedience.

- Punitive—their behaviors tend to blame, shame, humiliate, embarrass, and/or degrade young people.

- Demanding—based on parent's needs rather than the young person's capabilities.

- Unreasonable boundaries—fails to consider circumstances and what is and isn't developmentally possible for the young person.

DEVELOPMENTAL OUTCOMES FOR YOUTH OF AUTHORITARIAN CAREGIVERS

- They're not self-motivated. They fear making a mistake as it might invite ridicule from their caregiver.

- They have low self-esteem. They have experienced too many putdowns from authoritarian caregivers, which leaves them with negative self-esteem. This makes them easily led by peers because they want to fit in and be liked.

- They have lower cognitive skills because they're told what to do and what not to do. These youth are rarely given opportunities to think for themselves. They walk on eggshells, always afraid of upsetting the authoritarian caregiver.

STYLE #2: PERMISSIVE-INDULGENT

Motto: *"The world is my kid's playground!"*

CHARACTERISTICS OF PERMISSIVE-INDULGENT CAREGIVERS

Permissive-indulgent caregivers exhibit the following behaviors:

- Warm and nurturing.

- No or low expectations of youth.

- Allow youth to do whatever they want.

- Make excuses for a young person's inappropriate behavior.

- Fix situations, issues, and challenges for young people.

DEVELOPMENT OUTCOMES FOR YOUTH OF PERMISSIVE-INDULGENT CAREGIVERS

- Youth of permissive-indulgent caregivers have low emotional control because their caregivers have never required them to control their emotions.

- These kids are known as spoiled brats. They have poor social skills. They're not good at compromising, turn-taking, or following rules, because they have not been expected to.

These kids have low self-control because they have *not* been given the opportunities to develop self-regulation, which is needed for self-control.

Style #3: Avoidant-Uninvolved

Motto! *"I'm busy right now!"*

Characteristics of Avoidant-Uninvolved Caregivers

Avoidant-uninvolved caregivers exhibit the following behaviors:

- They have nothing or little to do with the young person.

- They make few demands, if any, of youth in their care.

- They demonstrate low responsiveness and have little communication with the youth in their care.

- They may or may not fulfill a young person's basic needs but are generally detached from the young person's life.

- In extreme cases, these parents may even reject or neglect the needs of their youth.

Development Outcomes for Youth of Avoidant-Uninvolved Caregivers

- High risk for NOT developing self-awareness skills.

- High risk for NOT developing a positive self-image.

- High risk for NOT developing a positive sense of self-esteem.

116

- High risk for NOT developing a strong sense of self-efficacy.

- High risk for NOT reaching their full emotional, social, creative, physical, and intellectual potential.

- They tend to look for love in all the wrong places.

- They may join gangs to establish a sense of family.

- They are more likely to drop out of school.

Please remember that if you have used some of the behaviors identified in one of the above less-desirable parenting or teaching styles, please don't judge yourself, berate yourself, or feel guilty. Be a model that mistakes are opportunities to learn. You can change and learn to choose strategies that reflect authoritative parenting and teaching styles.

A WORD ON SELF-DIAGNOSING YOUR CAREGIVING STYLE

The more you practice the strategies in this book, the better you'll become at implementing the authoritative caretaking style and avoiding these three impeding styles. But remember that while practice makes perfect, good practice requires toleration of imperfection. Make sure you forgive yourself if you're less than perfect in avoiding these impeding styles and in practicing authoritative caregiving—especially during your first year of practice. Also, give yourself permission to change your caregiving approach when you get it wrong. For example, when you find that you were too ridgid when disciplining your child's inappropriate behavior, it is acceptable to rethink your position and say "Given your age I may have been to ridged with my expectations why don't we practice loading the dishwasher together." Don't worry about whether your young person will judge you for this or think you weak, incompetent or indecisive.

Youth are very understanding. It is also good for them to discover that parents and teachers can make mistakes and that even adults can learn to do things differently. If you model a willingness to change your mind when necessary, you'll give your young person a powerful example to follow throughout *their* whole life.

Author's Summary and Perspective

In this chapter, we've discussed the relationship between development, learning and caregiving. As young people grow up, much of their development comes by learning from their primary caregivers. Young people are always learning. Whether they're absorbing information that helps or harms their development is a question we must continually ask. The extent to which we model appropriate behaviors, provide developmentally appropriate learning opportunities, and encourage youth to persist when the going gets tough, is the extent to which youth will go to think and act positively. Most importantly, we've discussed how young people are picking up messages from us every time we interact with them—whether they're aware of it or not. Some of these messages are subtle, others are obvious. But they all matter. So we should always consider our behaviors (including our caretaking style) as part of our communication.

Since we cannot deny the impact we have on a young person's overall perception of themselves. Here are a few questions worth asking:

- What happens to youth who don't experience good communication with their primary caregivers?

- What happens to youth who don't live in environments with secure attachment, authoritative caregiving, and positive youth guidance?

- What happens to youth who don't have appropriate role models, who are not given appropriate learning opportunities, and who rarely or never get support and encouragement?

We know that many of these young people are at risk for developing an unhealthy self-image. They're unlikely to have experiences which will assist them in building meta-self-awareness skills such as self-regulation, positive self-esteem, and a strong sense of self-efficacy. Consequently, these young people are at high risk for not developing optimistic thinking or the positive behaviors that will help them achieve their dreams.

CHAPTER 8:
THE BASIC TOOLS OF MEANINGFUL CONNECTIONS

In this chapter, we'll preview some basic tools for building meaningful connections with young people. This way you'll understand the psychology behind the strategies in the *Positive Youth Guidance System* (see Chapter 9). The tools summarized in this chapter help to build a positive self-image while simultaneously offering young people the learning opportunities to develop the skills of the five selves (intellectual, creative, emotional, social, and physical). These tools include:

- Behavior modeling
- Learning opportunities
- Encouragement
- Authoritative caretaking

We'll also cover the best parenting, discipline, and communication styles for building meaningful connections that will support and promote teaching and learning.

120

Each of these basic tools have been tested and proven to promote the best most positive outcomes for making meaningful connections with youth of all ages. This is why the *Positive Youth Guidance System* is comprised of these tools and includes practical and detailed examples. This way, you can start using them to build the meaningful connections your young person needs right now!

BEHAVIOR MODELING

Albert Bandura (2016), the father of social learning, identified "modeling" as one of the most powerful forms of learning. His work revealed how young people observe adults and imitate their behaviors. He explained that a person is more likely to repeat someone else's behavior if they see that *other* people have responded positively to it. It also revealed that a person is *less* likely to repeat someone else's behavior if they see that other people have responded *negatively* to it.

Imagine, for example, a group of young people sitting in a classroom. One kid raises their hand. The teacher responds "Great, we have a question. I like questions. It shows me that you are paying attention." All the young people sitting in that classroom will *learn* to model the student raising their hand because of the teacher's positive response (i.e., "It is safe for me to raise my hand; the teacher will see me in a favorable light"). Now, imagine the teacher responding to the kid's question with the following sentence, "If you'd read the assigned chapter last night, you would not need to ask a silly question!" Again, all the young people in the classroom would learn (from observing) that it's unsafe to ask questions.

According to Bandurian theory, caregivers should model the behaviors they want youth to learn. We've all heard the saying, "Youth learn from what we do, not what we say." But sometimes an adult's words and actions send mixed messages to young people. For example, a parent who tells his child that lying is wrong, and then lies in front of the child to purchase a discounted movie ticket, obviously sends a confusing message. They might as well be saying to the young person "lying is wrong unless it benefits us." Parents sometimes forget that young people are observing their every move. If we want our youth to be honest, we must model honesty. If we want our youth to be kind, we must model kindness.

Caregivers who want youth to develop a positive self-image must model the traits and characteristics of a positive self-image. This includes the positive modeling of behaviors associated with the three pillars of self-image: self-awareness (including meta-self-awareness and self-regulation), self-esteem, and self-efficacy.

LEARNING OPPORTUNITIES

John Dewey and Maria Montessori dedicated their life to the study of youth and learning. Their conclusions and research have withstood the test of time. They discovered that learning is best accomplished by doing. Adolescents need learning opportunities to develop and hone specific skills. Whatever skills we want our youth to learn, we must provide them with opportunities to learn them. Consider the following examples:

- Caregivers who want youth to discover their creativity will nurture the ideas of young people and provide them with opportunities to create in a variety of modalities (e.g., art, music, dance, acting, photography, programming, cooking, sports, poetry, design etc.).

- Caregivers who want youth to learn emotional skills provide youth with opportunities to identify the needs behind their emotions, and to determine what to do about them (e.g., coping strategies, calming techniques, nonviolent language, etc.).

- Caregivers who want youth to learn math provide youth with opportunities to practice math skills (e.g., adding, subtraction, multiplication, division, geometry, algebra, statistics, calculus, etc.).

- Caregivers who want youth to develop a positive self-image encourage youth to persist when challenges occur. They remind young people of their strengths and they accept their weaknesses. They make it easy for them to fail and to try again. They provide opportunities and experiences for young people to discover their own talents and interests and to change their minds. Most importantly, they love, like, and enjoy young people for their individual uniqueness.

ENCOURAGEMENT

Alfred Adler (2014), Rudolf Dreikurs and Pearl Cassel (1991) have received overwhelming support for their work on the positive impact encouragement has on young people's ability to persist in the face of challenges. Children who are encouraged develop a sense of belonging, which in turn secures their investment in themselves. Youth who are encouraged by adults will act in connected and cooperative ways. Encouragement helps youth feel capable and appreciated. But when youth are discouraged, they act in unhealthy ways (e.g., giving up, social withdrawal, wining at any cost, etc.). Youth need caregivers who respect them and who encourage them by valuing and supporting their social interests. This promotes hopeful and optimistic feelings in the young person. Youth who observe and receive encouragement also learn to express and to *accept* encouragement (Dinkmeyer & Dreikurs, 1965).

Persistence is defined as the quality that allows someone to continue doing something or trying to do something even when it is difficult or when others oppose it (*Merriam-Webster's Collegiate Dictionary*, 2016). Dr. Angela Duckworth of The University of Pennsylvania discusses persistence and grit as being a larger indicator of success than IQ. According to Duckworth, having passion for something provides us with the grit we need to persist. Grit adds the component of passion as a motivating factor to persistence. We all experience setbacks, but with persistence we reach our goals despite those setbacks, and despite our mistakes or challenges. Whether a young person persists in learning a skill despite previous failures is heavily dependent upon their caregiver's encouragement. Some caregivers encourage youth to persist, and others discourage youth by degrading, teasing, and putting them down. But caregivers who encourage youth during tough times give youth the freedom to learn by doing, failing, struggling, and/or starting over (Duckworth, 2017).

AUTHORITATIVE CARETAKING

Caregivers of adolescents go beyond parents, they include, school teachers, staff, and administrators, coaches, mentors, tutors, spiritual counselors, and volunteers who interact with youth daily. Parenting style is a pattern of attitudes caregivers exhibit toward young people. Based on these two dimensions Baumrind (1967) revealed three distinct parenting styles. Maccoby and Martin (1983) expanded upon Baumrind's work, creating a fourth style. These four parenting styles are:

- **Authoritative:** warm, nurturing, democratic, reasonable demands, expectations and boundaries.

- **Authoritarian:** cold, rigid, excessive demands and expectations (usually based on the parent's needs). Authoritarians are likely to use physical punishment, to withdraw kindness, to bully, to tease, or to put young people down.

- **Permissive/indulgent:** warm, nurturing, no boundaries, no expectations of their children...their kids are spoiled brats who have little to no self-control.

- **Negligent/neglectful:** disinterested in their children. In severe cases may even neglect child's physical needs.

Before we get too deep into discussing parenting styles, remember that our primary default caretaking style is the style that impacts youth the most and has long-term consequences. In other words, our parenting style can have a positive or negative effect on adolescents. Again, I want to remind my readers that the term "development" when used in this book always refers to the *whole person*—intellectual, creative, emotional, social, and physical, in addition to self-image and the pillars of self-image.

Diana Baumrind identified two broad dimensions of parenting/caretaking styles: One of these dimensions is referred to as *responsiveness vs unresponsiveness* and the other is *demanding vs undemanding*.

When using the first dimension—*responsiveness vs unresponsiveness*—we consider our response to the child's intellectual, creative, emotional, social, and physical needs. When using the—*demanding vs undemanding*—we are evaluating our demands on the child's intellectual, creative, emotional, social, and physical skills. We like to think about these terms as a scale with extremely responsive being a score of 10 and extremely unresponsive being a score of 0. Extremely demanding is scored as 10 whereas undemanding is a score of 0. Between 10 and 0 there are of course different scores, for example, somewhat responsive might be scored at 7 and somewhat demanding might also be scored at 7.

Authoritative parenting is the best style because it delivers the most meaningful connections with youth. Authoritative caregivers are responsive to the whole child. They have reasonable expectations of them and they set reasonable boundaries based on the youth's, temperament, age, intellectual, creative, emotional, social, and physical abilities. Authoritative parents are democratic. They give young people choices, and this demonstrates that they respect the young person and trust them to make their own decisions, and mistakes. Authoritative parents respond to mistakes by building connections that support and encourage youth to stop, think, and choose the right behaviors; behaviors that meet the young person's needs, while respecting the freedom offered to them by the adult.

Authoritative parents encourage adolescents when unforeseen challenges pop up. Children of authoritative parents view their parents as fair, respectful, and open-minded. But these kids are keenly aware that their misbehaviors also have a consequence. Authoritative parents do not threaten; they follow through with stated consequences. Unlike authoritarian parents, authoritative parents do not degrade, shame, humiliate, embarrass or withdraw love and affection from their teens. Unlike permissive indulgent parents, authoritative parents do not allow their adolescents to use them as door-mats and they don't make excuses for their children's bad behavior (Diana Baumrind, 1967).

Most people think of caretaking and parenting as respond-ing to youth's physical needs by keeping them healthy and safe. But Baumrind's responsiveness dimension goes beyond responding to a young person's physical needs. Responsive caregivers are in tune with youth's *emotional* needs and they respond appropriately. Responding to a young person's phys-ical needs is not enough! Like adults, young people need someone to respond to all of their needs (i.e., intellectual, creative, social, emotional, and physical needs).

Youth learn who they are from both covert and overt mes-sages their caregivers send them. And this learning begins at infancy. Imagine two infants crying. One gets a bottle while her caregiver is talking on the phone and giving her little or no attention. The other gets a bottle while her caregiver holds her, looks into her eyes, talks to her and comforts her with a calm, soothing voice. One child's physical needs are met with the bottle, but her emotional needs are unmet. The other child's social, emotional needs are met along with her physical needs. Both infants are learning about themselves from this experience with their respective caregivers.

Which caregiver sent messages which would build a posi-tive self-image? Which caregiver met the infant's emotional need for comfort and soothing? Which caregiver delivered the messages: "I care about your feelings," "Your feelings are important to me," "You are my priority," and/or "You matter to me." Too often we assume that since infants aren't using verbal language yet, they aren't getting these kinds of messages. But this is wrong.

One infant is learning that she is important, she matters and that she can signal her needs and have them met. As a result, the infant's self-evaluation becomes: "I'm worthy. I'm important. I'm significant." The infant is also experiencing and observing the behavior of her caregiver and is more likely to model similar behaviors later in life. The infant is also learning how to respond to people who signal their emotional needs. Most importantly, the infant is building empathy skills (through mental models) by these observations. If infants learn from caretaking styles, imagine what adolescents are learning or NOT learning from the adults who interact with them.

The relationship between caretaking, learning, and development cannot be denied. Caregivers' responses influence a young person's self-image development in either a positive or negative way. Quality relationships between youth and caregivers depend on the types of acceptance demonstrated by those caregivers. As early as 1967, Stanley Coopersmith's research showed that youth with negative self-esteem had mothers who gave them limited affection (non-responsive parenting type). Youth with positive self-esteem, however, had parents who were affectionate (responsive type). Parental warmth, acceptance, and reasonable boundaries promote

129

positive self-esteem. K.M. Enright and M.F. Ruzicka (1989) claim that parents who are willing to set clear boundaries and to explain to their children their reasons for disciplining them, boost their children's self-esteem as a result. All of these are examples of the authoritative caretaking style.

Edward Morvitz and Robert W. Motta (1992) indicated that youth's perception of both maternal and paternal acceptance was significantly related to their self-esteem. In the Global Journal of Human Social Science, Arts & Humanities, Cai-Lian Tam et al, reported that their research indicated a strong relationship between authoritative caretaking and adolescent self-efficacy. They found that adolescents with authoritative parents had stronger senses of self-efficacy when compared to adolescents with authoritarian or permissive parents. Self-efficacy is essential for self-confidence! Together, these two traits determine whether or not we "try" to accomplish a goal or task.

Overall, caretaking behaviors play a critical role in youth's development of self-awareness, self-regulation, self-esteem, and self-efficacy. Starting from the time their young people are born, caregivers will provide positive, negative, or neutral experiences. They also provide the environment and context within which a young person develops certain skills, and they do it in a way that is either appropriate for the young person's age and ability level, or inappropriate. Caregivers with authoritarian, neglectful or indulgent parenting—often without knowing it—do this in a way that inhibits the young person's development. But authoritative parents provide learning experiences which are interesting, and which take place in an emotionally positive and supportive atmosphere.

A Good Discipline Style

There are a variety of strategies caregivers can use to motivate young people to behave in ways that are socially acceptable. These strategies can be divided into four categories:

- Indulgent.
- Punitive.
- Ignoring.
- Positive Discipline/Guidance.

Indulgent Strategies. Caregivers using indulgent strategies have few boundaries and few expectations of youth. Instead, they want to be friends with them. They make excuses for the young person's inappropriate behaviors. They don't provide appropriate modeling, learning opportunities, or the type of encouragement that will foster a positive self-image. In social circles young people must use self-control to cultivate friendships (e.g., wait their turn, compromise, accept constructive criticism without having a meltdown, etc.). But young people with indulgent caregivers have low self-control because they're never given opportunities to practice the skill of self-control (Ferris, 2016; Henrick & Weissman, 2014). Needless to say, young people with low self-control rarely build deep, meaningful, respectful relationships with others.

Punitive Strategies. Caregivers using punitive strategies are poor role models for helping young people develop healthy emotional skills such as self-regulation and self-control. Punitive strategies do not encourage youth to persist, even though parents who use them believe that threats, teasing, embarrassing, humiliating, shaming, blaming, degrading, slapping, spanking, biting, hitting, kicking, punching, or the withdrawal of love, attention, or care will somehow motivate children. Instead children simply become afraid of making a mistake or messing up. Worse, is that punitive strategies cause physical or psychological harm to young people leaving them feeling worthless (Ferris, 2016; Henrick & Weissman, 2014).

Sometimes caretakers use punitive behaviors with good intentions in mind. Punitive caregivers resort to these behaviors because of their own unresolved issues. Nevertheless, indulgent and punitive strategies don't give youth the freedom to grow. Sherrie Campbell, PhD (2017), advises caregivers to find a balance between comfort and growth expectation. For example, having growth expectations means allowing youth to experience confusion and suffering as a part of their self-discovery process. Meanwhile, allowing for comfort means giving young people a place to get away from the confusion and suffering long enough to rest their mind and reflect on what they learned from it. Such a balance gives young people adequate opportunities for self-discovery so they can develop resilience and form a positive self-image.

Ignoring Strategy. An intentional "ignoring" strategy is used to guide child behavior, especially if the child is acting disruptively to get attention. In such a situation the parent knows the child is capable of doing something, but the child is being disruptive because they want the adult's attention. The parent who uses intentional ignoring is trying to send the child a message like, "I believe in you and I know you are capable of doing this on your own. I'm ready to look at it after you are finished." The child is learning that they will not be rewarded for disruptive behaviors.

Positive Discipline Strategy. The positive discipline strategy is also called positive youth/child guidance. This final strategy is what we should strive for. It relies on meaningful connections, focuses on keeping youth safe and healthy while offering learning opportunities and encouragement. This way, the young person can discover who they are (what they stand for) and what they are meant to do in life (purpose), while building a positive self-image, self-awareness and meta-self-awareness skills (self-regulation & self-control), positive self-esteem, and a strong sense of self-efficacy. Positive youth guidance is based on the beliefs that:

- Youth are innately good.

- Youth want to please adults.

- Youth want to be independent.

- Youth have their own individual needs and interests.

- Youth struggle to learn new things just like adults do.

- Youth are natural explorers who want to learn about their world (home, schools, community, etc.).

- Youth need learning experiences, warmth, understanding, and encouragement for healthy development, which includes developing a positive self-image.

Positive Youth Guidance is a discipline that respects developmentally appropriate practices (DAP). As youth grow and develop their intellectual, creative, social, emotional, and physical needs their preferences change. Caregivers who use DAP adjust their caregiving behaviors to match each child's temperament, interests, age, and abilities across five aspects of development:

- Intellectual/cognitive
- Creative
- Emotional
- Social
- Physical

Positive Youth Guidance is discipline that respects youth's need to belong and to feel significant. Once our needs for food, shelter, and safety are met, the primary need for all humans is a sense of belonging and significance. Belonging is our sense of where and how we fit in. Significance is tied to social interest—our ability to contribute to the world around us in meaningful ways, to find purpose. Young people who are encouraged and feel a sense of belonging and significance will behave in positive ways. But youth who are discouraged will exhibit misbehavior because they have a mistaken idea about how to find belonging and significance.

With *Positive Youth Guidance* caregivers can stop wondering whether they are too lenient, too strict, or too demanding. The positive atmosphere that results from us using positive youth guidance is apparent immediately. The energy spent scolding, yelling, punishing, being frustrated, being angry, and being confused is now spent supporting our kids in developing all that they need in order to live a truly good life.

We expect to teach our young people to know right from wrong, to follow rules, to be kind, to care for and respect themselves and others. We hope they do well in school, in the workplace, and in all endeavors that interest them. I suspect most of us want young people to do what we ask of them and behave as we expect them to, but we also want them to learn to think for themselves, make good choices, intercede on their own behalf, set goals and achieve them, take responsibility for their actions, and know how to cope with challenges. This means as adults we must make meaningful connections with them even when they are not behaving as the darlings we'd like them to be. By using positive youth guidance and turning a young person's missteps into learning opportunities through meaningful connections we provide the rich circumstances and opportunities they need to develop a positive self-image and healthy thinking habits.

Helping youth learn the rules of acceptable behavior, whether it be eating their vegetables, brushing their teeth, doing their homework, cleaning their room regularly, respecting their curfew, etc., requires young people to develop self-regulation and to use self-control. *Positive Youth Guidance* via meaningful connections does this. Self-Regulation empowers us to stop, think, and process the consequences of our behavior before we take action. But whether we take the appropriate action, depends on our capacity for self-control. And since all other types of skill development depend on our ability to self-regulate in this way, self-control is the pivotal skill of positive development.

When faced with a situation which requires child guidance, every caregiver must ask themselves, "What do I really want this child to learn?" Lauren Lowry (n.d.), clinical staff writer for The Hanen Center, suggests that in order for youth to follow rules and behave as adults expect they must develop self-regulation. Research on self-regulation, suggests that challenges take on a new perspective when trying to provide learning opportunities for young people. Shanker and Baker (2017) suggest that, when attempting to correct a nuisance behavior, we should momentarily take our focus off trying to modify the behavior, and consider how we can help the young person develop self-regulation. This is a better long term solution, because, in the long run, a young person will benefit more from the ability to self-regulate.

Lowry discusses the connection between behavior regulation and language. The ability to express wants, needs, preferences, anger, and frustration is critical for self-regulation because language is one way we assert ourselves without using aggression. In "What is Behavior Regulation and What Does it Have to Do With Language Development?" Lowry writes:

"Helping youth learn to regulate their behavior isn't about helping them learn to sit still, comply with directions, and control themselves. It's about providing an environment where young people can make choices, understand expectations, feel relaxed, burn off steam, and have energy left to face challenges in their daily life. This means trying to figure out the demands placed on the child, factors that help the child stay calm and alert, what the child does to control himself, and what causes a child to become under- or over-stimulated."

This is great advice, and backed up by solid research. The National Association of the Education of Young Children (NAEYC) and other experts in the field of child development agree that the best way to approach discipline is by using positive child guidance (Driekers & Cassel, 1991; Miller, 2016; Nelson, n.d.).

Of course, we know that it is impossible to create perfect environments for youth to live in every minute of every day. But we also know that there are times when a young person misbehaves, and we must learn to use these situations to benefit them as often as we can. We do this by making *Positive Youth Guidance* our default manner of thinking and acting when interacting with our young people. For example, when misbehavior occurs, we must remember to focus on the learning opportunity we can provide. Addressing misbehaviors this way will help the young person to develop self-regulation, self-esteem, and self-efficacy, all of which will foster a *positive self-image*.

To summarize, caregivers use *Positive Youth Guidance* when they look at each situation with the priority of helping the young person develop the five pillars of self-image. NAEYC suggests caregivers reframe each situation from the perspective of the youth, instead of simply reacting to youth's missteps. As the adult of the situation, remember to ask, "What is it I really want this young person to learn?" Young people's mistakes, missteps, and misbehaviors offer us opportunities to turn an unplanned situation into a learning opportunity. Telling young people what to do or what not to do is not particularly helpful long-term. But helping them build new knowledge for handling similar situations in the future will build their critical-thinking skills and help them self-regulate. We will cover some specific strategies for this in the *Positive Youth Guidance System.*

A Good Communication Style

Most of us know that communication is a skill. Like any other skill, it must be learned, but it can also be improved with practice. Most importantly, it deserves our time and our attention.

Sherrie Campbell, psychologist, Ph.D., presented an article titled "10 Things Youth Need Most from Us Parents" in the Huffington Post. Her list includes love, faith, confidence, patience, affection, counsel, compassion, guidance, respect, and time. These ten things are delivered to youth through our behaviors, and our communication style. We need to use good communication to deliver the intention of our messages accurately. How else can we know that the messages we send to our youth are messages of love, faith, and trust? We also use communication to show young people that we trust them to make good choices because we have witnessed their success with a specific task. This is a huge boost to the young person's self-confidence.

We love our youth and we want the best for them. Sometimes our young people present us with situations which we either don't understand or which we feel might bring them pain or suffering. For example, a young boy asks his parents to enroll him in ballet because he sees ballet as beautiful. The parents may refuse, saying to their son, "Ballet is for girls. Others will make fun of you and tease you. It is best if you choose a more masculine activity." This most often comes from love. The parents don't want their son to be hurt, teased or bullied. In fact, the parents probably view their behavior as protectively loving. But are these parents delivering a message that says, "We have faith in your choices and confidence that you can learn how to deal with teasing or bullying?"

Humans get hurt. They get teased and bullied. They fail, make mistakes, and mess up. Hurt, pain, disappointment, frustration, and anger are all part of life and cannot be avoided. Caregivers who know this understand that it is more effective to help youth develop appropriate coping strategies for dealing with life stressors. We humans learn from experience and we learn to deal with challenges by experiencing challenges. So caregivers must learn to prepare their young people for these challenges instead of trying to shelter them from every potentially painful experience. The best way to deliver messages that will help young people do this is to become a more effective communicator.

The overt and covert messages caregivers deliver to youth affect youth's self-image. What we say to youth delivers overt, explicit messages, and the way we say it (e.g., body language, tone) delivers covert, implicit messages. Note: Some caregivers ignore young people when they speak. Other times, they mutter meaningless phrases under their breath to pretend that they're listening, or they respond with silence and/or disapproving body language. All three of these disrespectful responses deliver negative messages to the young person. Imagine that you were trying to express an idea, an occurrence, or something meaningful to a friend. How would you want them to respond? You'd want them to listen and to understand your experience and feelings without judging you or giving you unsolicited advice. Youth want the same thing.

Adult caregivers often think a young person's expressions are a nuisance or an interruption to their adult world responsibilities. Sometimes this is true. Your child is expressing an idea, and you are trying to decide how to pay the rent or whether you should buy food or gasoline or how you should handle your obnoxious supervisor. These are real concerns which require attention because they have real life consequences. But consistently ignoring a young person's needs, including their need to communicate with you, has real life consequences too. The consequences just don't show up immediately.

Consistent negative messages delivered by primary caregivers, whether overt or covert, impact a young person's development on every level (intellectual, creative, emotional, social, and physical). They also affect the young person's self-image. When we respectfully listen and respond appropriately, we are communicating messages like, "I care about you, what you have to say matters because you matter, your opinions are important to me." When we don't respectfully listen and respond appropriately, we communicate harmful messages like, "Your opinions are insignificant, you are not worthy of my time and attention, I don't respect you, and I have more important issues to attend to!" These messages play a powerful role in the way young people value themselves.

When caregivers are too busy or preoccupied to listen and respond appropriately to a young person's ideas, concerns, and opinions, they can simply say, "I really want to listen to your ideas. I need to finish this report now. Let's sit together after dinner, when I can give you the attention you deserve." Caregivers cannot be expected to drop their responsibilities as soon as a young person wants to talk with them. They can, however, respond respectfully. Telling a young person to wait also helps them develop self-regulation—a pivotal and necessary skill to leading a life of their choosing. Having said this, please don't take this as a way to "get rid of" your child. Rather, when a situation requires this, treat it as an opportunity to show genuine interest in listening to them.

Sometimes in listening to youth, caregivers may object to, or have serious concerns about the young person's expressed preferences or interests. In these situations, caregivers using good communication skills will respond with love, empathy, and compassion. For example, they can take time to express and explore their concerns with the young person rather than simply saying, "You can't take ballet lessons because others will tease you." They can explore their child's interest in dance, enroll him in classes, and help him hone his coping skills in case he does get teased. It's best to support and encourage a young person's interests and to discuss ways to address potential hurtful situations which may arise.

Adults who care for youth and have concerns as to whether they're using good communication can also ask themselves these questions:

- Am I using bidirectional good communication?
- Am I using appreciative inquiry?

Bidirectional Good Communication, according to Croft (2016), is when both people talk and listen to each other with respect. Bidirectional good communication is more than hearing what another person is saying, it's being fully engaged (emotionally connected) with what they're saying. There are several aspects to bidirectional good communication, including:

- Brevity;
- Clarity;
- Confidence;
- Empathy;
- Friendliness;
- Listening (the "forgotten half" of communication.);
- Nonverbal communication;

- Open-mindedness; and
- Respect.

Appreciative inquiry is a communication strategy for recognizing or drawing out the good thinking, good intentions, good effort, and good work a young person has put into a situation. The caregiver essentially asks the young person to tell their story about what has been happening. Once the young person feels that their efforts have been valued, they might feel safe enough to open up and share their emotions. Appreciative inquiry is a door opener to have a deeper conversation about their thinking and about the working strategies he or she chooses. The caregiver can use this new information to guide the young person in problem solving and behavior. The caregiver might also realize what additional tools the young person needs in order to learn from an experience and to develop a desired skill. Through appreciative inquiry, the caregiver can learn things which will help them provide the young person with developmentally appropriate responses.

Nelsen et al. (2007) has done extensive research on using positive, communication in place of negative communication. Caregivers who use positive communication:

- Encourage youth to perform a task or engage in a specific behavior by making a request of them rather than a demand.
- Model positive communication.

- Offer learning opportunities for youth to practice and hone positive communication skills.

For example, you can request that a young person behave in a specific way or you can demand it. Most adults believe that telling, directing, or demanding a young person to engage in a specific behavior is acceptable. In many situations this makes sense. Particularly when it comes to safety or health issues. We aren't going to request our teenager attend school. We set up expectations of behavior in advance, before the school day. But imagine you have a headache. Your son's music is annoying you. Rather than demanding, "Shut that music off. It's way too loud!" You could make a request: "I need quiet to rest right now. Would you mind turning down the volume of your music?" The demand upsets you and your son, but the request keeps you calm and is more likely to encourage your son respond positively. An extra benefit is that you are (modeling) teaching your son a better communication style—a style that models respect, empathy, clarity, and concision.

I suggest using the "ABCD Method" of communication, found in Part B of the Positive Youth Guidance System to help your young person practice and hone positive communication skills. This is a great way to implement bidirectional good communication *and* appreciative inquiry while building critical thinking skills, positive self-image, self-regulation, self-control, confidence, and mutual respect between you and your young person. This method can be used with young children, preteens, teens, and young adults.

AUTHOR'S SUMMARY AND PERSPECTIVE

Ultimately, that is the purpose of the strategies in this book— to help young people discover who they were born to be and to teach them to *live* as their authentic selves. This could literally save their lives, and it will certainly make the world a better place for all of us. If you're ready to get started, you'll be excited to see what the next chapter holds. We will cover some specific strategies for this in the *Positive Youth Guidance System.*

PREVIEW TO THE POSITIVE YOUTH GUIDANCE SYSTEM

So now, we've laid a foundation for building extraOrdinary youth. We've talked about self-image, thinking habits, meaningful connections, the obstacles to meaningful connections and the basic differences between effective and ineffective parenting styles. You now know enough to make a dramatic difference in the lives of the young people you care for. But this is just the beginning of our journey. The next step is to put this knowledge to work until these strategies become second nature. This is why I created the *Positive Youth Guidance System.*

As I mentioned in the preface, childhood stress and trauma can make a life and death difference for young people—and the reality of these risk factors is more common and more chronic than you know. C.D. Bethel (2014) states:

"Adverse childhood experiences are common among U.S. youth, and as demonstrated in adult studies, have lifelong impacts that begin early in life."

The good news is that childhood trauma and stress don't need to permanently shape a young person's development. Families can learn and live by strategies that will dramatically reduce the traumatic and stressful events a young person is exposed to, while giving them the tools to recover and even learn from such events. By making these strategies second nature, you'll bring a new level of hope and clarity which will empower you and everyone in your family. This calls for a commitment to identifying at risk youth. It also calls for a commitment to building meaningful connections with all young people and helping them make a positive influence in the world by discovering and developing their true gifts and callings.

You're now equipped with the basic knowledge for making this happen. But it takes practice and patience. Most importantly, it takes a specific set of hands on strategies. That's exactly what I've designed the *Positive Youth Guidance System* to do for you. So let's get started.

Chapter 9:
The Positive Youth Guidance System

Part A: 12 Strategies for Building a Positive Self-Image

The Positive Youth Guidance System is a proprietary system developed by Dr. Kim C. Metcalfe. The system consists of 12 strategies for adults to use when interacting with young people ages 10 to 21. Each strategy describes the reasoning, benefits, objectives, and specific behaviors required for applying the strategy.

Young people who are recipients of these strategies will develop the skills to live the lives they deserve to live. In addition to these skills, they will have a finely tuned moral compass and be a positive influence to their family s, their community, their nation, and to the world. They will have everything that need to live extraOrdinary lives.

Please keep your eye on the prize as you work through each strategy. Our goal as adults who love, care for, and work with kids, including tweens, adolescents, and young adults is to provide the experiences and opportunities that help them develop the skills they need to live productive, ethical, meaningful, joyful lives. Skills take time to develop. To develop skills, kids need to practice them to hone them. Be consistent. Be committed. Be determined and together we can ameliorate suicide, depression, anxiety, addiction, helplessness, and hopelessness.

STRATEGY 1: AUTHORITATIVE CAREGIVING

HOW TO DEVELOP CONFIDENT AND SELF-RELIANT YOUTH

As covered in Chapter 7, there are four caregiving styles. Most caregivers use all four, but tend to favor one as their primary, and this primary style has the most significant effect on the overall development of the young people they care for. Authoritative caretaking is considered the "ideal" primary caretaking style because it yields the overall best outcomes for youth, which is why it is included as a Positive Youth Guidance Strategy. Cultivate this caregiving style with youth and you will surely foster independence and reasoning skills within them.

BENEFITS OF AUTHORITATIVE CAREGIVING

Overall authoritative caregiving fosters independence and reasoning.

- Young people become self-reliant, socially responsible, independent, and achievement-oriented.

- Young people develop positive attitudes, positive self-esteem, self-confidence, and strong self-regulation.

- Young people learn to think for themselves and to consider the reasons for rules.

OBJECTIVES OF AN AUTHORITATIVE CAREGIVER

A. Be warm, nurturing, responsive and flexible.

B. Place reasonable age and ability expectations and boundaries on youth.

C. Identify expectations and consequences in advance and administer fair, consistent, positive discipline.

OBJECTIVE A: BE WARM, NURTURING, RESPONSIVE AND FLEXIBLE

A caregiver who is warm, nurturing, responsive and flexible is one who is receptive to a young person's intellectual, creative, emotional, social, and physical needs.

Strategies for Achieving Objective A

- Guide your young person to *self-discovery—Use Strategy 11- The Identity Platform* to accomplish this goal. A young person needs to understand that there's more to life than adults' expectations of them. Young people have their own goals, dreams, values, and interests. The sooner they discover these, the more determined, resourceful and responsive they'll become. Nurture each young person as an individual with their own needs, ideas, and requests—Use Strategy 2 —Nurturing the Individual to accomplish this goal.

- Allow youth to express their opinions and encourage them to discuss options.

- Ask youth open-ended questions to help them discover solutions and strategies for helping themselves—this is different from telling them what to do.

- Use time-ins to explain your position, discuss issues, and invite youth to share their perspectives—create two-way dialogues.

- Demonstrate that you are listening to your young person (e.g., give them your undivided attention—put down your cell phone and look at them!).

- Take time to make a thoughtful decision—especially if your automatic response is no. Tell youth that you want to revisit an issue after you've had some time to think about it.

- Resist the urge to embarrass, humiliate, or tease youth when they struggle or express fears, this is the time they need warmth and nurturing.

  - For example, a child who accidently wets the bed should not be teased, and neither should a teen who is afraid of small dogs.

  - Be flexible when it makes sense—flexibility allows adults to consider circumstances rather than being tied to rules that sometimes can be broken in order to respond to a young person's intellectual, creative, social, emotional, and/or physical needs.

    - Example: Your young person is expected to do homework immediately after arriving home from school. However, it is snowing outside, which rarely happens in your town, and he wants to go outside and play with the other kids. You know routines are good for youth, and you prefer for your son to do his homework before leaving the house. *Relax* and let go. *Rules are meant to be broken occasionally.* By allowing your son to go outside, you are modeling flexibility and respecting his needs for recreation (physical needs), socialization (social and emotional needs), and creativity (playing in snow).

OBJECTIVE B: PLACE REASONABLE EXPECTATIONS AND BOUNDARIES ON YOUTH BEHAVIORS BASED ON THEIR AGE AND INDIVIDUAL ABILITIES

Knowing a young person's intellectual, creative, social, emotional, and physical skills based on their age; and demonstrated abilities in each of these areas allows caregivers to set reasonable expectations and boundaries for those in their care. This knowledge also assists adults in being a bridge for youth to acquire new knowledge and new skills—adults who understand the skills that youth do have also understand the opportunities they must provide to help youth hone those skills and learn new skills.

Strategies for Achieving Objective B:

- Use a *Developmental Milestone Chart* that identifies typical behaviors and skills of young people at different ages. Observe youth to determine their abilities—ask yourself, are their abilities typical, above, or below their same aged peers? Knowing a young person's abilities allows adults to have reasonable expectations and set reasonable boundaries—based on the skills a young person demonstrates.

  - There are other benefits of knowing a young person's skills too. Developmental knowledge helps adults understand what young people of different ages are capable of. For example:

- Kids younger than eleven-years do not think abstractly. They cannot understand analogies and metaphors.

- A two-year-old doesn't have the emotional self-regulation and self-control to sit still.

- Explaining the logical consequences of teen pregnancy and/or STDs will not stop tweens and teens from having sexual intercourse. Adolescents have what researchers term an "invincibility fable"—the belief that something bad or negative won't happen to them.

Note to Parents

Differences in abilities/skills between kids of the same age are typically due to the different learning opportunities each child had. For example, an "only child's social and emotional skills may not be as developed as a child with siblings. This is because siblings are usually expected to share, take turns, and compromise—these are consistent learning opportunities that an "only" child may not have. Do not have a meltdown if your child's skill development is behind one of their peers. Nor should you go around bragging that your child is a genius because he has a skill that is superior to his peers. Your goal as a caregiver is to help youth advance their knowledge and skill base.

OBJECTIVE C: IDENTIFY EXPECTATIONS AND CONSEQUENCES IN ADVANCE AND ADMINISTER FAIR, CONSISTENT, POSITIVE DISCIPLINE

Strategies for Achieving Objective C

- Identify expectation in advance.

- Identify consequence in advance.

- Be fair—discuss possible situations that might impede a young person's ability to meet identified expectations.

- Be consistent—Do not disregard the consequence other than when you know the expectation could not be met due to unforeseen circumstances beyond the young person's control.

- Use positive discipline—resist yelling, screaming, blaming, shaming, humiliating, degrading or embarrassing young people. Resist using demeaning statements such as, "I'm so disgusted in you." The goal of adults is to support youth in learning strategies that build self-regulation so they can do better in the future.

Situation: Your teen is going out with friends for the evening.

- **Identify expectation**—I expect you to be home by midnight.

- **Identify consequence**—If you choose to come home late, we will take away the time you exceeded curfew from your next outing.

- **Be fair**—If an emergency arises, I need a call from you letting me know your anticipated new time of arrival.

- **Be consistent**—If the emergency is beyond the teens control, be flexible but if not, be consistent with the consequence.

- **Administer positive discipline**—Remain calm. Deliver the consequence in a matter-of-fact way. "You are 35 minutes late. The next time you go out you will need to be home 35 minutes before curfew. Ask questions that help youth revisit their actions and choices, "what could you have done differently to make it home on time?

Fairness and consistency are sometimes confusing.

Use *fair discipline*—make sure the severity of the discipline matches the severity of the offense.

- **Example of *fair discipline*:** Imagine that your adolescent doesn't clean his room by your mutually agreed upon time. It is reasonable that your adolescent not be allowed to participate in any fun or choice activities until the room is clean. However, it is not reasonable that he loses all privileges for a month. In this case, the discipline is much more severe than the offense and therefore unfair. On the other hand, it is not reasonable that your child simply gets a five-minute lecture and be allowed to move forward with personal plans before the room is clean. In this case, the discipline is much less severe than the offense, and therefore, also unfair. This is what I mean when I say that the severity of the discipline should match the severity of the offense.

Be *consistent* with discipline—This means that when you set boundaries and lay out logical consequences, when your young person ignores those boundaries, it is critical that you follow through in enforcing the consequence.

- **Example of *consistent discipline*:** Let's assume you set your young person's curfew for midnight. You tell him that he has a fifteen minute grace period, but after that it will cost him his going out privileges for the following weekend. Your teen arrives home at 12:25 a.m. He has violated curfew and the grace period. The following weekend is the prom and he begs you to postpone his consequence to the following weekend so he doesn't miss prom. If you agree to his offer, you are not being consistent. I am not saying that there are never exceptions to a rule or consequence because I already said that there are.

As the parent or caregiver, you must weigh the pros and cons of giving in to your boundaries. When you become inconsistent with discipline you are NOT giving your teen the opportunity to think ahead, self-regulate, and make choices that allow him to succeed in life. But when you *are* consistent, you help your young person to understand consequences and to govern themselves according to the consequences they want to create. Remember this basic truth in life, we teach others how to treat us—including our kids, we teach them that what we say is or is not to be respected.

Strategy 2: Nurturing the Individual

How to Help Youth Take Responsibility and Stop Blaming Others

When caregivers nurture a young person's needs, ideas, and requests, they are nurturing the individual. This is the formula to help a young person become self-directed and resourceful. This is especially important if you need your young person to stop blaming others (outside circumstances etc.) and to start taking responsibility to build the life they want.

Nurture

Nurturing is the process of caring for and encouraging the growth or development of someone or something. Youth who are nurtured feel safe, secure, and valuable which provides the bases for learning and healthy development.

Benefits of Nurturing

Adults who nurture a young person's needs, ideas, and requests deliver the following messages:

- You matter to me.

- You are important to me.

- I have confidence in you and what you bring to the table.

- Young people who feel safe, secure, and valued try new things and persist which supports learning.

- Young people who know that they're valued by adults are more confident in themselves, which promotes, evokes, and elicits self-directed behaviors.

  - Self-direction is a critical element in a youth's ability to intercede on his or her own behalf and remain true to who they are and what they stand for.

OBJECTIVE OF NURTURING THE INDIVIDUAL

OBJECTIVE A: NURTURE YOUTH'S NEEDS, IDEAS, AND REQUESTS

To nurture youth's needs, ideas, and requests, you must be clear on what those needs, ideas, and requests are. The nurturing adult takes time to listen and clarify what youth are expressing.

Strategies for Achieving Objective A

- Nurture the need for young people to express themselves and to be heard.

  - Make sure the message you're hearing is the message your young person is trying to communicate.

- ◆ For example, repeat your young person's messages back to them in their own language ("So, you want me to stop 'talking to you like you are two-years-old' in front of your friends? How can we communicate better when your friends are around?").

- Nurture your young person's ideas and requests.

  - Ask clarifying questions which demonstrate curiosity about your young person's needs, ideas, and requests.

    - ◆ Examples: "I'd like to hear more." "How can I support you best?" "What do you need next, what would make a difference?"

  - Use the "language of choice," as opposed to talking about things as if they're inevitable.

    - ◆ For example, "That's an interesting choice. Have you considered any other choices?"

- Cultivate a mind-set of *observation*—without judgment!

  - What did the young person say or do to reveal (directly or indirectly) their needs, ideas, and/or requests?

- Reframe and replace negative and/or judgmental language with clear and proactive language:

- "Should" or "shouldn't" are usually a sign of negative and/or judgmental language. For example rather than say, "You shouldn't do that" or "You should do it like this," you might say something like "You could try_____."

• Express "scary honesty" when you observe mistakes (make *certain* the timing is right!).

- For example, a child makes a Mother's Day card for his or her mom. Mom notices that there are misspelled words in the message of the card.

  ◆ Replace statements such as, "The card is lovely, but there are so many misspelled words," with, "I'm enjoying this card that you wrote for me." This is *not the time* to express concern with spelling errors.

  ◆ As another example, your child makes a card for Grandma or Grandpa. You notice misspelled words. Ask "Do you want me to check your spelling?" If they say, no, respect the response. "Okay. The card is beautiful, and I'm sure Grandma is going to appreciate your work and effort."

Note: Again, remember you'll have plenty of appropriate opportunities to correct their spelling.

STRATEGY 3: POSITIVE YOUTH DISCIPLINE

HOW TO TURN REBELLIOUS YOUTH INTO CHEERFULLY COOPERATIVE YOUNG ADULTS

There are different ways to respond to youth's missteps and inappropriate behaviors. Some adults ignore these behaviors. Others punish (blame, shame, humiliate, embarrass) young people for making mistakes. But caregivers who use positive youth discipline understand how to turn challenging situations into powerful learning opportunities for young people.

POSITIVE YOUTH DISCIPLINE

Positive youth discipline uses the language of love, support, and opportunities to encourage appropriate behaviors, while building critical life skills, and a positive self-image.

- Benefits of Positive Youth Discipline.
- Self-starting behaviors.
- Positive self-image.
- Self-regulation.
- Self-control.
- Confidence.
- Positive self-esteem.
- Strong senses of self-efficacy.

OBJECTIVES OF POSITIVE YOUTH DISCIPLINE

A. Set the mood & environment.

B. Listen then ask.

C. Replace assumptions with questions.

D. Tell your young person what you *need* instead of telling them what you don't want.

E. Give choices instead of giving commands.

F. Set boundaries and expectations which match your young person's age and ability level.

G. Catch your young person being good.

OBJECTIVE A: SET THE MOOD AND ENVIRONMENT.

Set the *mood* and set up the *environment* to create a supportive communication atmosphere.

Strategies for Achieving Objective A

Set the mood: The worse time to have a discussion is when the adult or the young person is angry. It's good to say, "We need to have a discussion about _____, but now is not the time because I am angry and need to calm down." When you both are angry say "...because we are both upset and need to calm down."

In times that demand immediate communication adults and young people can use the "Red Rule" for instant calming.

Use the "red rule" or some other coping strategy to calm yourself before reacting in anger.

- Red rule is a deep breathing and tapping technique for calming oneself. Put your hand over your heart, take a deep breath through your nose, slowly exhale the breath through your mouth, and at the end of each breath, tap your index finger against your chest and silently count one. Repeat until the index finger has tapped five times.

Set up the environment: setting up boundaries and expectations in advance eliminates a lot of problems in the future.

- Set clear, consistent, age and ability appropriate limits.

- Set goals that foster self-esteem and independence.

- Demonstrate respect. Youth learn to respect those who set limits and boundaries.

- Let your young person know when safety is the reason for a rule. Youth like to know that caregivers are looking out for them.

- Provide consistent limits and boundaries to clarify your expectations.

- Trust your young person to learn limits, boundaries, and consequences by setting them in advance and adhering to consequences. For example, "all cell phones are left in the kitchen on the charger before going to bed. The consequence for ignoring this boundary is limiting your phone use to emergency calls to limited numbers." There are many apps that allow parents to control phone usage.

  - The cool aspect of setting boundaries, expectations, and consequences up in advance is that when a boundary is crossed adults remain calm and cool. Simply remind the young person of the consequence. No lecture, no shaming, no blaming, no screaming or yelling. "You crossed the boundary and you know the consequence. Give me your phone, I need to put the controls on."

OBJECTIVE B: LISTEN THEN ASK

When kids misbehave it is critical to understand their perspective by active listening (e.g., drawing forth information instead of trying to stuff it in). When we actively listen during challenging times with our kids, we glean insight to their developmental limitations and needs. Consequently, we can offer them learning opportunities to improve their skills. By listening and asking questions we guide a young person in self-reflection (exploring their choices and behaviors). This helps them reflect on their choices and behaviors—the bad and the good!

Dad: Your teacher emailed me and said she was concerned that you haven't turned in homework last week. I need to know why.

Teen: I don't know.

Dad: You have been given more freedom but with more freedom comes more responsibility. You can choose to talk about this now or give me your phone until you are ready to talk.

Teen: You know I need my phone.

Dad: I respect that you believe you need your phone. I'm asking you to respect that as your father I need to find out why you aren't doing your homework. I'm ready to listen.

Teen: It's a bunch of new math that I don't understand.

Dad: What are some of the ways you could get extra help?

Teen: I asked my teacher, but I still don't get it. None of the other kids understand it either.

Dad: Do you believe when something is difficult it's a good idea to give up?

Teen: But I know I'm never going to need that math.

Dad: You might not need the math, but do you think it's a good idea to give up when something is difficult? What happens when there is something that is difficult that really matters?

Note: Notice that the goal of dad's conversation is to provide opportunities for his teen to self-reflect on her choices and behaviors. Self-reflection is a skill teens need to develop to succeed in life.

This process would not be possible if dad had begun with "Your teacher emailed me and said she was concerned that you haven't turned in homework for a week. I'm taking your phone away until you get that work turned in."

Objective C: Replace Judgments or Assumptions with Questions

1. **Judgment or assumption:** "You are procrastinating. Go do your homework! **Question:** "What do you need to get your homework done?"

2. **Judgment or assumption:** "I saw your room last night and it is filthy! You aren't going anywhere until it's clean." **Question:** "Have you cleaned your room this morning?"

3. **Judgment or assumption:** "You are failing English because you aren't trying." **Question:** "What can I do to support you in bringing your English grade up?"

4. **Judgment or assumption:** "I do not like Sarah's attitude. I do not want you hanging around with her." **Question:** "I'm curious, why do you like being with Sarah?"

5. **Judgment or assumption:** "You are one hour late and there is no excuse for it." **Question:** "Please explain why you are home one hour after our agreed upon curfew."

6. **Judgment or assumption:** "I'm the parent and you're the child, you have no right to raise your voice at me." **Question:** "Why are you raising your voice? What are you feeling right now, and what do you need?"

After asking the question and listening to their response, you can decide on a consequence whose severity matches the severity of the offense. During this interaction, asking youth, how they could have done something differently helps them stop and explore their thoughts (ideas)—this supports development of self-regulation, increases their cognitive processing skills, and helps them discover solutions to future problems.

OBJECTIVE D: SAY WHAT YOU NEED, NOT WHAT YOU DON'T WANT

1. **What you need:** "I need you to stay home and do your homework before going out." **What you don't want:** "I don't want you going out until you finish your homework."

2. **What you need:** "I need you to clean your room." **What you don't want:** "Don't go out until you clean your room."

3. **What you need:** "I need your plan for improving your school grades." **What you don't want:** "Don't you ever bring home these low school grades again!"

4. **What you need:** "I need you to describe what you like about Sarah." **What you don't want:** "Don't ever bring Sarah to our house again. I saw her smoking outside."

5. **What you need:** "I need you to tell me why you are one hour later than your curfew." **What you don't want:** "Don't you ever come home after curfew again or there will be serious consequences."

6. **What you need:** "I need you to lower your voice, so I can hear you." **What you don't want:** "Don't yell when you speak to me."

The purpose of expressing your need calmly and with warmth is to open the door to assess or evaluate situations before allowing your anger or your young person's anger to eclipse a learning opportunity. No one can argue against us when we are stating our need. By stating your needs you are also modeling healthy communication skills *and* supporting your young person's self-regulating skills.

You and your young person have different needs. By clearly stating *your* needs, you're making sure your young person doesn't feel personally attacked for their choices or behaviors. Most importantly, you're helping them understand that other people have different needs and that it's important to see situations from the other person's perspective.

OBJECTIVE E: GIVE CHOICES VERSUS COMMANDS—WHEN POSSIBLE OR WHEN IT MAKES SENSE

The objective in giving a choice is to, in a matter-of-fact way, state the *obvious* choice. When comparing the choices and commands below, you'll notice that the goals of each are almost identical. Yet, speaking within the context of choice sounds less condescending and makes for a friendlier communication. This is how the language of choice eliminates unnecessary power struggles.

Choice vs. Command

1. **Choice:** "You have a choice, go out for one hour, return, and do your homework, or do your homework and stay out for two to three hours." **Command:** "You will do your homework first, and then you are free to go out."

2. **Choice:** "You have a choice, clean your room and then you are free to go out or ignore your room and stay indoors." **Command:** "Clean your room first, and then you can go out."

3. **Choice:** "The choice is yours, use your phone during family dinner and lose phone privileges for a week or

put your phone away and keep your phone privileges. **Command:** "Give me your phone."

4. **Choice:** "You have a choice, you limit your social media time to one hour a day, or I can help you by putting parental controls on that limit your time." **Command:** "I've set parental controls on your phone because I don't trust you."

5. **Choice:** "You have a choice, limit your gaming to one hour a day, or I can help you by using parental controls." **Command:** "I put parental controls on your gaming device because I do not trust you to follow the rule."

6. **Choice:** "You have a choice, lower your voice so I can listen to what you are saying, or we will wait until you can." **Command:** "I'm your father and you will not raise your voice to me."

OBJECTIVE F: SET BOUNDARIES AND EXPECTATIONS THAT MATCH YOUR YOUNG PERSON'S AGE AND ABILITY LEVEL

Each child has his/her own temperament and intellectual, creative, emotional, social, and physical abilities. Considering this, it's important to set boundaries and expectations which are appropriate to your young person's age and ability level.

Strategies for Achieving Objective F

- Check "developmental milestones" (you can find these online) for all ages to get a real sense of what is and what isn't possible for a specific age group.

- Remember, every young person has different intellectual, creative, social, emotional, and physical skills.

- It is critical to understand that teens, although they appear to live in adult bodies, are not yet capable of processing information the way we do.

  - For example, youth are trying to discover who they are and establish their identity accordingly. In addition, the frontal lobe of their brain is not fully developed until they're twenty-five years old. Since the frontal lobe is where decisions are made, teens will frequently make decisions without considering all facts. This will continue until their brains have fully matured—so keep this is mind when setting your expectations.

OBJECTIVE G: CATCHING YOUTH BEING GOOD

The best time to reinforce a good behavior in a young person is when you catch them doing it. This way, This way, you can use process praise, which encourages them to repeat the behavior in the future..

Strategies for Achieving Objective G

1. **Situation:** Youth hangs his/her coat up. **At home:** Kyle, I noticed that you hung your coat up. You are doing a good job of remembering. **In the classroom:** I noticed that Kyle is remembering to hang his coat up.

2. **Situation:** Youth completes his/her homework. **At home:** Justina, you did your homework right after school. Now you have all evening to hang out with your friends. **In the classroom:** I noticed Justina completed her homework. I know it was a difficult homework assignment.

Things to Remember About Positive Youth Discipline

-   Youth don't have the knowledge and/or comprehension that adults have.

-   Youth are often busy exploring their environment to understand it. Exploration is needed for learning—caregivers don't want to discourage youth's natural inquisitive nature.

-   When youth are punished, they lose their natural desire to explore and to engage in self-starting behaviors. This can unknowingly impede learning opportunities and encourage more nuisance behavior.

Positive Youth Discipline helps youth build important skills such as self-regulation, which supports them in becoming *competent and independent.*

Strategy 4: Being the Encourager

How to Help Your Young Person Quit the Habit of Giving Up

Encourage youth when they want to give up because of difficulty or challenges that arise. A great way for adults to create a habit of encouragement is to use it consistently to develop persistence, and two other much needed characteristics in youth: 1. Integrity, and 2. Self-assertion.

Encouragement

To encourage is to give hope, confidence, and support. Encouragement helps young people persist with sustained effort which supports them in reaching their goals. Young people who experience reaching goals because they persisted through challenges are motivated to persist in the future in order to reach new goals. Young people who reach their goals feel proud of themselves *and* their accomplishments. Encouragement is a win, win for youth, adults who care for them, and society.

ENCOURAGEMENT TO PERSIST, LIVE WITH INTEGRITY, AND SELF-ASSERT ALLOWS YOUTH TO LIVE THE LIVES OF THEIR CHOOSING

PERSISTENCE

Whenever youth hit a bump in the road, that is the time they need encouragement to persist—which helps them reach their goals. To reach goals and dreams young people must be encouraged to use sustained effort particularly when the going gets tough. When we encourage youth to persist, we are giving them a rare opportunity to understand their purpose and why they matter as members of society.

Adults can also use encouragement to help youth develop personal qualities that are not taught in schools or extra-curricular activities such as, integrity and self-assertion. To develop and maintain these qualities youth must be encouraged to practice and hone specific skills. Young people are unlikely to build these skills without encouragement from well-meaning adults.

INTEGRITY

Living with integrity means our thinking, actions, and behaviors are aligned with our values and beliefs. To live in alignment youth must know who they are and demonstrate the actions and behaviors that reflect who they are consistently in all areas of their lives (e.g., home, school, work, community). In our society we rarely discuss the definition of integrity, how to maintain integrity in our lives, and the meaning, purpose, or power of living life with integrity. Telling young people to be kind, to be honest, to be truthful, to be fair, or follow the golden biblical rule of, "do unto others what you would have them do unto you," isn't enough, particularly when so many adults around them clearly do not live like this.

We live in a world that often ignores bad behavior and in which bad behavior is often rewarded. Our kids see corruption on every level—politicians, clergy, teachers, college administrators, and others in power. They also see that there are different rules for the wealthy and the rest of the population. Therefore, more than ever before the integrity conversation must become mainstream—and those responsible for developing our youth must encourage integrity.

SELF-ASSERTION

Youth with self-assertion skills can stand up for their beliefs and values. Being true to themselves promotes a young person to like and respect themselves. Youth who like and respect who they are have an internal dialogue that says I am worthy of reaching my goals and dreams—they persevere because they believe in themselves.

BENEFITS OF ENCOURAGEMENT

DILIGENCE

Young people who receive encouragement while doing a task, work harder, do better, and make more of an effort to complete the task at hand—even when challenges prevent them from doing well.

SUCCESS

The more encouragement youth receive, the more likely they are to succeed at their endeavors, which leads to a fulfilling successful life. The magic formula: Encouragement equals persistence equals success.

SUPPORT

Encouragement is one of the best ways to support youth, particularly when they struggle.

POSITIVE SELF-IMAGE, POSITIVE SELF-ESTEEM, SELF-REGULATION, SELF-CONFIDENCE, AND A STRONG SENSE OF SELF-EFFICACY

Youth who are encouraged are more likely to persist and therefore succeed in meaningful work and tasks. These successes contribute to a positive self-image, positive self-esteem, and self-confidence. The process of persistence builds critical skills such as self-regulation. The more a young person succeeds the more confidence they develop and the more belief they have in their innate ability to achieve goals.

OBJECTIVES

    A. Encourage sustained effort—Persistence.
    B. Encourage youth to live a life of integrity.
    C. Encourage self-assertiveness.

OBJECTIVE A: ENCOURAGE SUSTAINED EFFORT—PERSISTENCE

To encourage consistent, sustained effort means to encourage your young person to use continuous, steady, unremitting behaviors to achieve a goal.

Benefits of Sustained Effort— Persistence

- Adults understand that setting goals is relatively easy but reaching them is much more challenging. One goal might require an individual to reach a dozen sub-goals first. It takes sustained effort to reach each of these sub-goals. Without sustained effort, we can't reach our goals. And if we can't reach our goals, we can't live our dreams.

- Sustained effort empowers youth to live the lives they choose and want to live.

Strategies for Achieving Objective A: Behaviors that Encourage Sustained Effort

Remind youth of a time when you saw them use consistent, sustained effort to succeed at something (walking, talking, feeding, tying shoes, writing, reading, riding a bike, etc.). You can also use statements that empower youth while also encouraging persistence:

- "If you'd like, we will take one step at a time and practice."
- "Let's do it together."
- "I can help you or you can do it on your own."
- "You can say no, it's up to you."
- "Your choices matter."
- "Your words are powerful."
- "Your actions are powerful."
- "Your emotions may be powerful."
- "Trust your instincts."
- "Your ideas are worthwhile."
- "You are capable."
- "Failing gives us the power to try it a different way, practice more, or ask for help."

If your young person complains that something is "too hard" or "impossible" or that they'll "never learn it," remind them that almost everything that's easy for them today was once extremely difficult for them to learn (walking, using the toilet, talking, tying their shoes, memorizing their address or phone number, learning how to use different applications on their phones or computers, etc.).

OBJECTIVE B: ENCOURAGE YOUTH TO LIVE A LIFE OF INTEGRITY

We encourage integrity by providing opportunities for youth to explore, discuss, and identify their values and beliefs, and showing them how to use their values and beliefs to make easy to complex decisions.

Integrity is more about consistency and wholeness than it is about being "good." Being a good person is important, but we need to understand that it is categorically different from living a life of integrity. Integrity means to live in a way that is *consistent* with your personal values.

Benefits of Living a Life of Integrity

Young people with integrity:

- Are unique and rare as it takes inner strength to live a life of integrity;
- Know who they are and what they stand for which provides a roadmap for the way they live their lives, the choices they make, and the decisions they choose;
- Live a life with purpose—A meaningful life;

- Have confidence as an individual—they do not need to be fearful of getting caught in a lie, hide, or pretend because they are living a life with honesty;

- Build positive, healthy relationships where people are more willing to work and relate with you;

- Are respected by others;

- Are valuable to the self and others;

- Are protected against false accusations—People know who they really are because they are the same in all situations and with their words, and actions;

- Are trusted; and

- Draw others who live a life of integrity to them—those who live outside of integrity will avoid them because it is uncomfortable to be in their presence.

Do your best to guide youth in aligning their thoughts, words and actions. Demonstrate a strategy that helps them use their values, beliefs and virtues to think, choose behaviors, and make decisions. Remind youth that being liked because we pretend to be something (e.g., kind, honest, helpful) we really aren't, means that our likeability is based on a false self—and in their own mind they will know this truth.

Remind youth that we undermine our self-esteem when our outer personality doesn't express who we know ourselves to be. Our conscience knows the truth of who we really are. If we betray it, it will find a way to show others the truth—and it will remind us of the truth because we will not feel worthy of the good things that happen to us and we will self-sabotage. When we know what we stand for (values, beliefs, virtues), and our decisions and behaviors are aligned with what we stand for, we are true to ourselves, and we like ourselves.

Strategies for Achieving Objective B: Behaviors to Encourage Living a Life of Integrity

The best way to encourage integrity is to model it. This means that as caregivers we must:

- Know what *we* stand for.

- Be able to identify our own virtues quickly and without help from others (if you can't do this, then you don't know what you stand for).

- If you're going to **talk** the **talk,** you've got to **walk** the **walk.**

  - Young people notice your moral habits, including your casual speech, your attitudes, and your behaviors. All of these should align with your personal virtues. You can't claim to be kind if you gossip and belittle others.

  - Caregivers encourage youth to embrace and use personal virtues when discussing their moral beliefs and how those beliefs influence their decisions.

- Ask youth "moral questions" to encourage empathy and moral development. For example:

  - "How would you feel if someone treated you that way?"

  - "What would happen if everybody acted that way (e.g., stole, yelled, and/or cheated)?"

- Encourage youth to be as honest as possible when speaking or thinking about their chosen virtues.

- Encourage youth to be as honest as possible (in speech and thought) when evaluating whether their virtues are *really guiding their behaviors.*

- Encourage youth to discover what they stand for (virtues) and their life purpose (See the *Identity Platform* in Strategy 11). Encourage them to be true to these virtues and to live their purpose every day. For example:

  - Encourage them to identify three virtues that resonate with them.

  - Encourage them to use strategies that align their virtues with their daily behaviors. This will empower them to be true to themselves and to like themselves.

  - Encourage youth to apply their virtues to themselves. For example, the virtue of kindness is applied to others but being kind to themselves is equally important. The same is true for the other virtues. Being honest with oneself is equally important to being honest with others.

- Below is an example of a situation where a young person's decisions and behaviors move them toward or away from their chosen virtues. Decisions and behaviors that move them toward their virtues are the behaviors in which they are being true to themselves or standing up for their values and beliefs.

  ◆ A group of students is teasing/bullying another student. Ask youth to think about their virtues and apply them to possible responses that could be made in the situation. "I'm kind so I could speak up for the student being teased," or "I could go get help for the student," etc. The goal is to help them differentiate between responses that support their virtues and responses that contradict their virtues.

- Encourage your young person to fix and/or apologize for their personal mistakes. Youth who do this learn to take responsibility for their decisions and actions, rather than playing the blame game. Remind youth that by taking responsibility, they empower themselves to do it differently the next time. But that they give their power away when they blame others, because they can't change anyone but themselves.

Warning: Context Matters When Practicing Integrity

Practicing integrity requires understanding the context of our words and our actions. Otherwise, we'll be confused as to which virtue we should honor in a certain situation. For example, let's assume you've chosen honesty, kindness, and courage as your three personal virtues. Now, imagine your friend is trying on an outfit in a store. She asks, "does this outfit make me look fat?" If your answer is yes, you are being true to the virtue honesty, but you are not being true to your virtue of kindness. But ask yourself which responses would demonstrate honesty *and* kindness? You might say, "I think another dress would be more flattering." It is important to give young people opportunities to choose their virtues, but adults must also support them in being true to their virtues, and strategies to deal with these types of situations.

Regarding context, it's also important for your young person to understand that if their virtues involve meeting the needs of others, they must understand those needs from the *other person's* frame of reference. For example, what one person perceives as kindness might be perceived as coddling by another person. The same is true when defining and demonstrating love, respect, tenderness or trust. To practice virtues in a genuine social context means to understand how different people interpret these basic human needs.

OBJECTIVE C: ENCOURAGE SELF-ASSERTIVENESS

Being self-assertive is the ability to stand up for yourself, your beliefs, and your personal truths. Self-assertiveness is neither passive nor aggressive. It is a balanced response which requires self-confidence and self-regulation.

It gives youth and adults the confidence to express their thoughts, emotions, beliefs, and opinions effectively and honestly. We encourage self-assertiveness by providing youth with opportunities to explore, discover, and choose their own values, beliefs, and virtues and most importantly showing them ways to use these in everyday situations. *Applying Strategy 11 The Identity Platform* provides these opportunities.

Benefits of Self-Assertiveness

Youth who are self-assertive:

- Feel better about themselves;

- Have positive self-image;

- Have positive self-esteem; and

- Are skilled at protecting their rights and standing up for their personal values, beliefs, and virtues without undermining the rights of others.

Tip: Being assertive is not the same as being aggressive. Aggression means a forceful action, such as an unprovoked physical or verbal attack, especially when intended to dominate or master, whereas assertiveness means standing up for what you believe.

Strategies to Achieve Objective C: Behaviors to Encourage Self-Assertion

- Encourage youth to be reliable, truthful, and honest when interacting with others.

- Encourage youth to be true to the person they are regardless of whether others will accept them.

- Encourage youth to stand up for themselves and their ideas in appropriate ways.

- Encourage youth to use calm and concise responses to repeat their personal truth, rather than trying to defend it. Young people who own their values don't feel the need to justify them to everyone who demands an explanation.

- Encourage youth to resist arguing with those who oppose their opinions or their personal truths—their personal truths don't need to be *right* in the eyes of others.

- Encourage youth to self-assert their beliefs and values rather than comply with others. If you want to raise a child who can stand up for his/her beliefs, then reinforce assertiveness, not conformity and compliance.

Tip: Remind youth that self-assertion involves repeating their opinion, truths, feelings, and point of view, time and time again, without raising their voice or becoming angry, irritated, or distracted by pointless debates over who is right. Keeping a journal can help with this, as it allows a young person to explore and refine the contents of their own mind without fear of outside judgment or rejection.

STRATEGY 5: ACKNOWLEDGMENTS THAT MATTER

HOW TO TURN A LAZY YOUNG PERSON INTO AN INDUSTRIOUS YOUNG ADULT

Caregivers use the power of their spoken words to reveal their unconditional positive regard for a young person's accomplishments. This plants seeds of self-worth within young people. When these seeds blossom, young people recognize and embrace their unique qualities and characteristics. Think about this: Can anyone see themselves as valuable and worthy of unconditional love, support, and respect if their accomplishments are not celebrated?

ACKNOWLEDGMENTS THAT MATTER

Providing recognition with acknowledgments that matter means identifying specific qualities about your young person's work or efforts.

BENEFITS OF ACKNOWLEDGMENTS THAT MATTER

- Shows youth that you are paying attention to their individual contributions to a product, task, or situation.

- Young people feel valued for the qualities they bring to a situation, and feeling valued cultivates their confidence.

OBJECTIVES

A. Know the difference between meaningful acknowledgments and empty praise.

B. The magic is in the specifics. Use acknowledgements that matter.

STRATEGIES FOR ACHIEVING OBJECTIVE A: KNOW THE DIFFERENCE BETWEEN ACKNOWLEDGMENTS THAT MATTER AND EMPTY PRAISE

Acknowledgments that matter are those that *praise the process* a young person uses (e.g., "Good job! You must have worked really hard to finish.)" Empty praises are those that *praise the person* (e.g., "Good job! You are really smart.").

- An acknowledgement that matters will showcase the young person's creativity, choices, efforts, individuality, uniqueness, and decision making.

- Empty praise is praise that is general and doesn't highlight the person's accomplishments. Telling a person that they did a good job because they are smart will lead them to believe that when they do not do a good job it is because they are not smart enough. We want to praise effort because we want our kids to understand that with effort, they can accomplish their goals.

STRATEGIES FOR ACHIEVING OBJECTIVE B: MEANINGFUL ACKNOWLEDGMENT VS EMPTY PRAISE

To use acknowledgments that matter your words must showcase the young person's creativity, choices, efforts, individuality, uniqueness, or decision making. Below are some examples that compare acknowledgements that matter with empty praise.

Meaningful Acknowledgments

Meaningful acknowledgments provide a reason for the acknowledgment and focuses on the quality of the work or the process.

Empty Praise

Empty praise gives no reason for the acknowledgment. It focuses on the person.

1. **Meaningful acknowledgment:** "Wow, you solved that problem by thinking outside of the box." **Empty praise:** "Good job!"

2. **Meaningful acknowledgment:** "I'm proud that you thought to call your sister for help when you couldn't reach me." **Empty praise:** "I'm proud of you."

3. **Meaningful acknowledgment:** "I know it was a difficult decision, but you took the time to think it through." **Empty praise:** "You made a good decision."

4. **Meaningful acknowledgment:** "I like that you didn't give up even when it was difficult." **Empty praise:** "You did it! I'm proud of you."

5. **Meaningful acknowledgment:** "You did it by yourself, and it took effort." **Empty praise:** "All done—good work."

6. **Meaningful acknowledgment:** "I like that you are brave enough to try something new with your hair." **Empty praise:** "You look very pretty."

7. **Meaningful acknowledgment:** "I think that pink shirt goes really well with that green jacket. I would never have thought to put those colors together." **Empty praise:** "You look handsome."

8. **Meaningful acknowledgment:** "You practiced and practiced, you didn't give up and your ball catching has

really improved." **Empty praise:** "Great ball catching today!"

9. **Meaningful acknowledgment:** "You stuck with it and concentrated and that's great." **Empty praise:** "You are such a great student!"

10. **Meaningful acknowledgment:** "You tried many different strategies and you figured it out." **Empty praise:** "You are smart I knew you would figure it out."

Strategy 6: Cultivate Confidence

How to Turn a Timid or Antisocial Young Person into a Sociable Young Adult

Environments which cultivate confidence are safe and allow for youth to explore and to learn by trial and error.

Confidence

Confidence is a feeling of self-assurance arising from one's appreciation of their abilities and/or qualities. What if you could cultivate a strong sense of confidence in all youth you care for?

THE ROLE OF ADULTS IN CULTIVATING CONFIDENCE

- Adults are the architects of a young person's environment.

- Adults who support youth in their choices are adults who trust and have confidence in a young person's ideas and interests. How do you build confidence in yourself when no one has confidence in you?

  - Adults who support young people's choices show those choices to be worthy. This helps the young person build internal confidence.

  - Adults who cultivate an "environment of choice" demonstrate their confidence in young people as individuals with their own needs, values, and beliefs.

BENEFITS OF CONFIDENCE

- Confidence is at the core of everyone's ability to advocate on their own behalf.

- Internal confidence encourages young people to stand by their choices and to say *no* without fear.

- Internal confidence empowers youth to be trusting, decisive and transparent.

- Young people who are confident are more likely to be assertive, positive, engaged, enthusiastic, and persistent.

OBJECTIVES

A. Make it safe for youth to express themselves and to be heard.

B. Use trust and choice to support confidence development.

C. Develop and/or restore confidence.

OBJECTIVE A: MAKING IT SAFE FOR YOUTH TO EXPRESS THEMSELVES AND TO BE HEARD

Create an environment of safety, whether in the classroom, home, or elsewhere. This will nurture young people's thoughts and choices.

Strategies for Achieving Objective A

- Let youth know that you want to hear their fears and reasons for doing or not doing something. "You are in a safe zone. That means you can express your thoughts and I will hear you."

- Support youth when they express concerns about failing or "messing up."

  - "What is the worst thing that can happen?"

  - "The only true failure is failing to try, or letting failure stop you."

- "I have failed many times before I succeeded, but eventually I succeeded, and you can too."

- Discuss all of the inventions that we use today and the many failures of inventors before they got it right. "It's normal and okay to fail."

- Replacing limiting beliefs—when a young person expresses doubts about their ability to succeed at something, introduce a belief that supports confidence, "Think about a time you doubted your ability to get something done but you did it."

OBJECTIVE B: USE TRUST AND CHOICE TO SUPPORT CONFIDENCE BUILDING IN YOUTH

Trusting youth's choices builds their confidence.

Strategies for Achieving Objective B

- Give choices when appropriate. For example:

- "We are going to the beach today. Would you like to stay home or go with us?"

- "This is a school night. If you want to go to a movie, what time do you think you can be home and ready for bed?"

- Trust your young person's choices by giving them what they need in order to succeed.

- "I see you are disappointed in your friend. What do you think you need, and how can you get that need met?"

- "Which extracurricular activities are you interested in?"

- "I loved playing football in high school, but that doesn't mean you will. If you choose to join the math club, I respect your choice."

- "You can change your mind. Why don't we talk about it?"

OBJECTIVE C: DEVELOP AND RESTORE INTERNAL CONFIDENCE

As adults we know what it is like to lose confidence in ourselves. When youth lose confidence, it is important for us to support them in restoring it.

Strategies for Achieving Objective C

- Break difficult tasks into steps. Notice effort rather than the end result.

- Be practical. If confidence is shaken due to social or emotional circumstances, assist youth in practicing skills that will help them succeed in similar situations.

WARNING: RESIST THESE COMMON TEMPTATIONS

- Resist the urge to push your preferences on youth.

- Resist the urge to compare youth to each other.

- Resist the urge to label youth. Labels can sound complimentary, but sometimes they put youth in box that they feel stuck in. For example, when kids are good at something, and receive lots of compliments they may come to believe that the compliments will go away if they try something else that they are not so good at—this is scary for some kids. They may also feel obligated to stick with activities they are praised for, because to quit would be letting their parents, coaches, and/or teammates down. Read the following example to understand the difference between labeling a youth versus acknowledging their current interests in a positive way.

  - "This is Sophie, our star soccer player." A better statement is, "This is Sophie. She loves to play soccer. If you enjoy soccer, you may want to go to one of her games one day."

Strategy 7: A New Way

How to Make Your 'No One Understands Me' Young Person Feel Valued and Understood

Adults who connect, acknowledge, and accept youth's feelings without judgment empower youth to discover coping strategies. These strategies help young people work through powerful feelings and challenging situations. Imagine supporting a young person's social and emotional intelligence by giving them tools that empower them in their daily life. In time, they will develop habits that will follow them into adulthood, and persist for the rest of their lives.

- *When you connect* with youth's feelings without judgment, you encourage them to pursue open and honest communication with other adults.

- *When you acknowledge* youth's feelings without judgment, you help them recognize those feelings as valuable indicators of an unmet need.

Benefits of Connecting, Acknowledging, and Accepting Feelings without Judgment

- We honor youth's individual choices.

- We teach young people that their feelings are acceptable, but that their actions must still be respectful of others. Physical or verbal harm to the self or others is inappropriate, unacceptable, and intolerable.

OBJECTIVES

A. Separate feelings from behaviors.

B. Connect, acknowledge, and accept *feelings* without judgment.

OBJECTIVE A: SEPARATE FEELINGS FROM BEHAVIORS

Adults who separate a youth's feelings from their behavior can then accept the feelings and reprimand the behavior. This is important because appropriate emotions can still lead a person to inappropriate behaviors. It is never one person's job to tell another person how to feel. As caregivers, it is our responsibility to support young people in learning to use appropriate responses when they experience strong emotions.

BEHAVIORS TO CONNECT, ACKNOWLEDGE, AND ACCEPT YOUTH'S FEELINGS WITHOUT JUDGMENT

SITUATION 1

Your teen has been caught cheating on an exam in school.

Adult: "Tell me why you felt the need to cheat on the exam."

Teen: "I didn't want to fail another exam."

Adult: "What is another way to ensure you'd pass your exam?"

Teen: "I could study more ... but I just don't understand this stuff!"

Adult: "Am I correct to say you were in fear of failing and your need to pass led you to cheating?"

Teen: "Yes."

Adult: "I understand your fear. There are appropriate choices to address your fear. Cheating is not one of those choices. Your need to pass your exam is admirable, but cheating is not."

Consequences for the above situation could focus on a new plan to manage the fear of failing *and* to prevent cheating in the future. For example, you might say, "This weekend you will remain in the house and develop a solid study plan to prepare for your next exam. You will write your teacher an apology and express your feelings and why you felt the need to cheat. You will also provide me and your teacher with a written study plan to ensure your readiness for the next exam. You will show me what you did to satisfy your study plan every day."

Tips:

- Notice that the adult in the above situation accepts the fear but does not approve of the cheating behavior.

- Notice that the adult remains focused on identifying a solution that addresses the need behind the cheating behavior.

SITUATION 2

Your teen says: "I hate you!" or "I hate him/her!" or "I hate my teacher!"

First, take your best guess on what feeling your teen is expressing.

Adult: "It sounds like you are feeling angry. Is that true?"

Teen: "Yes!"

Adult: "What happened to make you so angry?"

Teen: "My teacher is so unfair. She gave us a test, and it didn't have any of the stuff she had us read to prepare for the test."

Adult: "You are angry because you have a need for fairness. Is that correct?"

Teen: "Yes!"

Adult: "Do you have any ideas of appropriate ways to address your need?"

Hint: Notice in this dialogue the parent is helping the teen identify his or her feeling and the need attached to it. This strategy forces the young person to engage the frontal lobe. The limbic system is the seat of emotions and we do not want to "act" before we connect the limbic region with the frontal lobe of the brain where decision making, judgment, and reasoning occurs. In other words, we are engaging youth in a process that prevents them from taking action based on pure emotion without any reasoning—which we all know dooms us to ineffective behaviors that typically make a situation worse.

STRATEGY 8: OFFER MEANINGFUL WORK

HOW TO HELP ANGRY, FRUSTRATED, OR ANNOYED KIDS FIND PEACE AND SATISFACTION

Imagine empowering youth by offering them meaningful work and providing them with tools that help them to succeed and to master it.

MEANINGFUL WORK

- Meaningful work is satisfying, rewarding, enjoyable, and supports a healthy state of wellbeing.

- Meaningful work should be appropriate to a young person's age and abilities.

- Learning to take pleasure in work is discovered by doing work.

- We can start laying the foundation that work is satisfying and rewarding as early as four years old.

- Youth who become adults with the belief that work is oppressive and demeaning will have a difficult time in life.

BENEFITS OF MEANINGFUL WORK

- Meaningful work builds intellectual, creative, emotional, social, and physical skills.

- Meaningful work supports young people in developing a sense of mastery, autonomy, independence, and confidence.

OBJECTIVES FOR MEANINGFUL WORK

A. Offer meaningful work.

B. Assist youth in developing steps to succeed in meaningful work.

C. Provide supportive materials and opportunities for youth to master meaningful work.

While it is critical that adults offer meaningful work to young people, what matters most is helping them gain a sense of mastery in their accomplishments.

OBJECTIVE A: OFFER MEANINGFUL WORK

Offer meaningful work by offering opportunities that are not overly challenging *or* excessively easy. If the activity is overly challenging, youth will get discouraged and give up. If it is too easy, youth will get bored and give up.

Strategies for Achieving Objective A

- Offer work that is meaningful for the age and ability of youth.

- Offer work that is meaningful for the interests of youth.

- Offer work that is meaningful for a youth's natural talents.

- Offer meaningful work that can be divided into steps.

- Encourage, encourage, encourage for greater successes.

OBJECTIVE B: ASSIST YOUTH IN DEVELOPING STEPS TO SUCCEED IN MEANINGFUL WORK

The way to tackle more complex tasks and situations is to break learning goals into manageable steps. The best learning is accomplished by succeeding in many small steps. For example, if we want to paint a room, we must first select the paint and paintbrushes. Then we prepare the room (tape, pull furniture away from the walls, cover the furniture, etc.).

Strategies for Achieving Objective B

- Use paper, pencil/pens, and discussions to assist youth in developing a step-by-step plan to accomplish large tasks that will give them a feeling of accomplishment once completed.

- Celebrate the learning that a young person achieved through each step of the process. This will help young people value and enjoy the process of working and not just the end result.

OBJECTIVE C: PROVIDE SUPPORTIVE MATERIALS AND OPPORTUNITIES FOR YOUTH TO SUCCEED IN MEANINGFUL WORK

Having the right tools and opportunities can make a big difference between success and failure. Sometime, that "tool" or that "opportunity" can develop a skill that is developed through focused practice.

Strategies for Achieving Objective C

For young children, provide tools that are the right size for small hands and small bodies. These tools assist youth in achieving independence and self-care (e.g., feeding oneself, toileting oneself, grooming oneself). Some examples include:

- Small cartons or small plastic pitchers to aid youth in pouring drinks for themselves

- Small eating utensils and a divided plate with a suction to help youth succeed in self-feeding

- Small writing tools and wide-lined paper to help youth succeed in writing and coordination

- Books with words in large print and words that youth can learn easily (e.g., color words, number words, rhyming words).

For preteens and teens, calculators, computers, library cards, books, access to virtual libraries, tutors, mentors, field trips, and other tools and opportunities can help them succeed in academic tasks and goals involving their personal interests. For example, a teen wants to audition for a specific role in the school play, rather than saying "good-luck" or "I think you are good enough to get the part," you might say "How can I support you in delivering the audition you envision?" Perhaps your teen would benefit from a specific "tool" (video camera) or an "opportunity" to increase practice. Your job is to be open and supportive of providing meaningful work and the tools and opportunities that promote success in the work.

Strategy 9: Imprinting

How to Give Your Young Person a Deep Sense of Personal Empowerment

Imprinting

An imprint is an image produced by pressing a hard object into a softer one; for example, feet leave imprints in the sand, fingers leave imprints in soft clay or in cookie dough. In the current context, imprinting means to imprint specific behaviors into a young person's mind by modeling those behaviors yourself.

Youth learn by observing. What youth see is what youth do. This means, you should demonstrate the characteristics you want to imprint into youth. Even the most stubborn young person can argue with your words, but they can never argue with your actions. This is what makes modeling one of the most powerful teaching tools.

Benefits of Imprinting

- Imagine the actions you demonstrate as the cornerstones of your young person's future.

- Remember that these actions will become your young person's behaviors at home, in the classroom, in social situations *and* (eventually) in their workplace.

- Imprint it so they learn it!

OBJECTIVES OF IMPRINTING

A. Imprint positive self-image.

B. Imprint self-regulation.

C. Imprint positive self-esteem—includes taking responsibility for choices and actions; and self-assertion.

D. Imprint a strong sense of self-efficacy.

OBJECTIVE A: IMPRINT POSITIVE SELF-IMAGE

You can imprint a positive self-image by demonstrating a positive self-image. Self-Image is the mental image we have of who we are and how we show up in the world. This mental image includes our perception of our intellectual, creative, emotional, social, physical skills and abilities, and our appearance. Our perceived strengths and weaknesses are also part of our self-perception.

Benefits of a Positive Self-Image

- Your perspective of yourself is a key component to high performance in all kinds of situations. That's because this perspective influences your thinking, decisions, and behaviors and therefore, what you get out of every situation. Only when you believe yourself capable of accomplishing something can you find the courage to give it a try.

- A positive self-image provides a positive, optimistic framework or lens to your thinking.

- Positive, optimistic thinking leads to positive behaviors.

- Positive behaviors lead to positive outcomes.

- Young people with positive self-images become adults with positive self-images, and thus with positive, optimistic thinking habits.

Strategies to Achieve Objective A: Imprint a Positive Self-Image

The most powerful strategy to imprint a positive self-image in a young person is to demonstrate *your* positive self-image using the following behaviors:

- Emphasize the positive rather than negative in your personal life.

- Respond appropriately to strong emotions (use self-regulation and effortful self-control).

- Engage in behaviors that repair and nurture you, particularly in challenging situations.

- Accept compliments without shame.

- Show excitement when learning new knowledge and an eagerness to listen to different perspectives.

OBJECTIVE B: IMPRINT SELF-REGULATION

You can imprint self-regulation by demonstrating self-regulation. Self-Regulation involves examining your emotional state and identifying the need related to that emotion.

Benefits of Self-Regulation

- Self-Regulation is an important skill that supports you in getting the need attached to a strong emotion, met appropriately. When you tune into your emotions you use your "emotional meter" to identify a specific need. This links the emotional state to self-empathy (e.g., I have a need and I can make decisions and choose behaviors to get my need met). By using your efforts to get your need satisfied, you avoid letting your emotional state inhibit your self-control.

- One key component to high performance is your ability to self-regulate using *self-control*. This requires you to regulate your emotions.

- Self-Regulation allows you to understand and to meet your daily needs. You'll have various needs throughout your daily life. These needs can be tangible (e.g., shelter or food, etc.), or intangible (e.g., love, respect, understanding, etc.). Since emotional stress is the result of not satisfying these intangible needs, they are just as important as your tangible needs.

- An emotion is a signal of an unmet need. Think of this as your sixth sense. Beyond touching, smelling, hearing, seeing, and tasting, we feel. Our senses are meant to support our physical health and safety, but our emotions support our emotional safety. As we navigate through life, we are protected through our ability to scan our environment, *fight, flight, or freeze*. Likewise, we are protected by our ability to "feel" our unmet needs, and self-regulation allows us to get our unmet need met appropriately. Allowing emotions to move you before you self-regulate can result in emotional outbursts or shutdowns, sabotaging your efforts to get your needs met.

Empathy as the Key to Imprinting Self-Regulation

The most powerful strategy for imprinting self-regulation is to use empathy to demonstrate your own self-regulation. Empathy defuses the powerful drive behind emotions—a drive that sometimes causes us to behave in ways that hurt others. This sabotages our own ability to get the need met that has caused the strong emotion. Emotional outbursts such as anger, frustration, grief, or fear, in adults and youth, always stem from an unmet need. Get the need met or addressed with empathy and the strong emotions are ameliorated.

Strategies for Achieving Objective B: Imprint Self-regulation Using Empathy

Identify the feeling with a word, identify the need with a word, then pose the need as a question. Empathy only occurs when a feeling word and a need word are connected and agreed upon.

Tuning into the Feelings and Needs of Others Using Empathy

Situation 1

A parent is feeling an intense emotion (e.g., anger, frustration, disappointment) because their teen, for the third week in a row, didn't clean his room according to the scheduled time.

Response using empathy: "Our agreement is that you clean your room every Tuesday. Could you be feeling overwhelmed because you have too much to do now on Tuesdays? Do you need to choose another day?" **Response without empathy:**"I am sick and tired of reminding you to clean your room, clean it now!"

Situation 2

Your young person is angry about his grade. Your goal is to use empathy and try to get him to identify the need attached to his anger. Note: This isn't always easy but stick with it. Notice how the adult in the following situation ends the conversation—by never getting angry and giving up on the goal.

Adult: "Could you be feeling angry about your math grade because you need to do well in your school work?"

Youth: "No!"

Adult (rephrasing the question): "Could you be feeling embarrassed of your grade because you need to feel capable?"

Youth: "No!"

Adult: "What do you believe you need?"

Youth: "I don't know!"

Adult: "Why don't we work together to figure it out so you can get that need met?"

Youth: "I don't want to talk about it!"

Adult: "We have discussed the purpose of identifying the need attached to strong emotions. When you are ready, I'm here to help you."

If, after two attempts, you can't identify your young person's feelings and needs, you might say, "I really want to understand how you are feeling and what you need."

The goal of imprinting is to serve as a model for young people to observe. When youth see parents and teachers identifying and connecting feelings and needs, they learn to do it too.

Summary of Imprinting Self-Regulation with Empathy

- By using empathy, we defuse a potentially emotionally charged outburst that does little to actually solve a problem, and in fact often sabotages us from getting what we really *need*.

- Remember, self-regulation is tuning into our own emotional state and identifying a specific unmet need. This is a skill that requires practice.

OBJECTIVE C: IMPRINT SELF-ESTEEM

Imprint positive self-esteem by demonstrating positive self-esteem.

Self-esteem is our personal judgment of what we are worth. We express this judgment by evaluating our traits, characteristics, and roles in society. For example, if our self-image includes our belief that we are "very talkative" our self-esteem is our evaluation of the trait "very talkative." Do we believe "very talkative" is a strength or weakness? If we believe "very talkative" is a strength, our self-esteem moves in a positive direction. However, if we believe "very talkative" is a weakness, then our self-esteem moves in a negative direction.

Our self-esteem is based on our overall evaluation of who we perceive ourselves to be. Positive self-esteem means we have a favorable evaluation of ourselves (our traits, personalities, etc.) whereas negative self-esteem means we have an unfavorable opinion of ourselves.

Benefits of Positive Self-Esteem

Positive self-esteem is a key component of high performance:

- Positive self-esteem promotes the belief that we are capable of making decisions that will help us reach our goals.

215

- Positive self-esteem supports our internal belief that we are worthy of reaching our goals and dreams.

Strategies to Achieve Objective C: Imprint Positive Self-Esteem

- Engage in tasks that showcase your competence.

- Act independently also referred to as self-assertion (e.g., not influenced or controlled by others).

- Take responsibility for your thoughts, emotions, and behaviors (resist blaming).

- Work through your own frustrations effectively.

OBJECTIVE D: IMPRINT A STRONG SENSE OF SELF-EFFICACY

Imprint a strong sense of self-efficacy by demonstrating a strong sense of self-efficacy. Self-Efficacy is your belief in your ability to succeed in specific situations or to accomplish a task. Self-Efficacy plays a major role in how you approach goals, tasks, and challenges.

Benefits of Self-Efficacy

- Your belief in your ability to accomplish a task and to reach desired goals is a key component of high performance.

- People with strong senses of self-efficacy develop deeper interest in the activities they participate in. They also form stronger commitments to their interests and activities.

They recover from unexpected setbacks and frustrations; and they see a challenge as something to be accomplished or mastered.

Strategies to Achieve Objective D: Imprint Self-Efficacy

- Share your action plans with your young person.

- Stay committed to the things that matter to you, especially when challenges arise.

- Demonstrate your ability to recover from unexpected setbacks and frustrations.

- Demonstrate your commitment to accomplish your goals by taking one step at a time.

IMPRINT VIRTUES

Wanting young people to be virtuous isn't good enough. Adults must demonstrate the virtues they want youth to develop.

BENEFITS OF VIRTUES

- Know what *we* stand for.

- Be able to identify our own virtues quickly and without another people's help (if you can't do this, then you don't know what you stand for).

- If you're going to **talk** the **talk**, you've got to **walk** the **walk**.

- Young people notice your moral habits, including your casual speech, your attitudes, and your behaviors. All of these should align with your personal virtues. You can't claim to be kind if you gossip and belittle others.

- Caregivers encourage youth to embrace and use personal virtues when discussing their moral beliefs and how those beliefs influence their decisions.

- Ask youth "moral questions" to encourage empathy and moral development. For example:

  - "How would you feel if someone treated you that way?"

  - "What would happen if everybody acted that way (e.g., stole, yelled, and/or cheated)?"

- Encourage youth to be as honest as possible when speaking or thinking about their chosen virtues.

- Encourage youth to be as honest as possible (in speech and thought) when evaluating whether their virtues are *really guiding their behaviors.*

- Encourage youth to discover what they stand for (virtues) and their life purpose (See the *Identity Platform* in Strategy 11). Encourage them to be true to these virtues and to live their purpose every day.

STRATEGY 10: SMART ENGAGEMENT

HOW TO TURN YOUR YOUNG PERSON'S ANGER OR FRUSTRATION INTO ENTHUSIASM

Imagine being able to turn your young person's anger, inappropriate behaviors or missteps into unique learning opportunities. This is what smart engagement does—it turns potentially explosive situations into a magical opportunity for dialogue and collaboration between you and your young person.

SMART ENGAGEMENT

Smart engagement uses "feelings based" and "needs based" words and statements to replace anger with calm, apathy with enthusiasm, worry with certainty, anxious with calm, and frustration with cooperation.

A LEARNING MOMENT

A learning moment is a set of events that makes it possible for a young person to create a memorable experience. This long term strategy empowers the young person to retrieve what they have learned years, or even decades after the learning moment has taken place.

Benefits of Smart Engagement

- Smart engagement is the best way to support youth in building self-regulation and self-control.

- Smart engagement provides strategies that calm strong emotions.

- Smart engagement provides strategies that support youth in getting their unmet needs met.

- Smart engagement supports emotional well-being.

What Happens to Our Bodies when Strong Emotions Arise within Us?

Our bodies use our emotions to inform us and to protect us in our environment. There are approximately 297 molecules of emotion (neuropeptides) in the body. These molecules shift from moment to moment to inform our bodies of a wide range of stimuli, triggers, and dangers. The purpose of these molecules is to "move" us into action to get the need attached to the emotion met. For example, when our bodies feel tired, they need rest. The *feeling* of *tiredness* is a neuropeptide telling us that we need rest. In other words, the *need* for *rest* is causing the neuropeptide to activate within our body.

When we have a strong emotion, we are living in that emotion, and it clouds our judgment and ability to get what we really need. For example, when we are angry, we are in the state of anger, and we aren't looking at solutions. Only when we step outside of our anger and ask ourselves, "Why am I angry, and what is my anger informing me of? What do I need?" are we ready to find a solution.

OBJECTIVES OF SMART ENGAGEMENT

A. Smart engagement to teach, *labeling the emotion* as a calming technique.

B. Smart engagement to teach, *identifying where the emotions lives* in the body to maintain calm.

C. Smart engagement to teach, *identifying needs* and *getting needs met appropriately.*

STRATEGY OBJECTIVE A: SMART ENGAGEMENT TO LABELING EMOTIONS AS A CALMING TECHNIQUE

The fastest and best way to help youth calm strong emotions is to help them step outside of the emotion. This is achieved by encouraging youth to practice connecting their physiology to their language. The first practical step to achieve this connection is to ask youth to use the word that best describes their feeling (emotion).

Strategies to Achieve Objective A: Calming Technique

- Post a word list of emotions in the house or the classroom in order to introduce and give easy access to the many words we can use to describe our feelings.

- Teach young people to use the word that best describes their emotion, when a strong emotion presents itself. Explain to youth that emotions are a sign that they need something. And labeling the emotion allows them to calm themselves and move toward getting their need met. Remind youth that this is a powerful tool that keeps them in charge of their own actions and getting their own needs met.

  - The minute the young person begins to decide the word that describes their emotion they engage the frontal lobe of their brain where reasoning and judgment happen. Now their frontal lobe is connected to their limbic system (seat of emotions) and they aren't ruled by pure emotion, which doesn't get their need met.

- Imprint healthy calming techniques

  - Use the words posted to describe your own strong feelings.

  - Break the habit of responding like a robot when asked "How are you?" Responding with "I am fine" cannot possibly accurately describe our feelings every time the question is posed. People use this default response because they do not believe the person asking the question wants the truth. The problem is, however, these default answers remove us from our real feelings. It is okay to say, "I'm sad at this moment," or "I am frustrated but working through it."

OBJECTIVE B: SMART ENGAGEMENT TO TEACH TO TEACH IDENTIFYING WHERE THE EMOTIONS LIVE IN THE BODY TO MAINTAIN CALM

Maintaining calm is accomplished by keeping youth engaged in connecting their physiology to their language. Teach young people to describe where the emotion is living in their body—this process maintains calm while keeping youth connected to their frontal lobe. Remember, connecting the frontal lobe, where reasoning occurs, to the limbic system, where strong emotions emit chemicals throughout the body, is critical before taking action. More importantly, this is the process of self-regulation—thinking about and analyzing our own thoughts and possible outcomes of different behaviors before we take action.

Strategies for Achieving Objective B: Maintaining Calm

- After youth use the word to describe their feeling (emotion), ask them to describe where their body feels the emotion (e.g., head, heart, throat, stomach, chest, neck, shoulders, etc.).

- Imprint maintaining calm by describing where you feel your emotions after you describe your feeling with a word. "I feel disappointed that I had to cancel meeting my friends today, I feel it in my chest."

Categories of Feeling Words

A

1. **Disgust**
2. Embarrassed
3. Exposed
4. Guilty
5. Ignored
6. Inadequate
7. Incompetent
8. Inhibited
9. Inept
10. Inferior
11. Insignificant
12. Sick
13. Shame
14. Squashed

15. Stupid
16. Ugly
17. Unaccepted

B

1. **Happiness**
2. Adored
3. Alive
4. Appreciated
5. Cheerful
6. Ecstatic
7. Excited
8. Glad
9. Hopeful
10. Jolly
11. Jovial
12. Joyful
13. Loved
14. Merry
15. Optimistic
16. Pleased
17. Satisfied
18. Tender
19. Terrific
20. Thankful
21. Uplifted
22. Warm

C

1. **Anger**
2. Aggravated
3. Accused
4. Angry
5. Bitter
6. Cross
7. Defensive
8. Frustrated
9. Furious
10. Hostil
11. Impatient
12. Infuriated
13. Insulted
14. Jaded
15. Offended
16. Ornery
17. Outraged
18. Pestered
19. Rebellious
20. Resistance
21. Revengeful
22. Scorned
23. Spiteful
24. Testy
25. Used
26. Violated

D

1. **Sadness**
2. Alone
3. Blue
4. Burdened
5. Depressed
6. Devastated
7. Disappointed
8. Discouraged
9. Grief-stricken
10. Gloomy
11. Heart-broken
12. Hopeless
13. Let down
14. Lonely
15. Miserable
16. Neglected
17. Pessimistic
18. Remorseful
19. Resentful
20. Solemn
21. Threatened

E

1. **Fearful**
2. Afraid
3. Alarmed
4. Bashful

5. Cautious
6. Frightened
7. Haunted
8. Helpless
9. Hesitant
10. Horrified
11. Insecure
12. Lost
13. Nervous
14. Petrified
15. Puzzled
16. Reassured
17. Reserved
18. Scared
19. Sheepish
20. Tearful
21. Uncomfortable
22. Useless

F

1. **Surprise**
2. Astonished
3. Curious
4. Delighted
5. Enchanted
6. Exhilarated
7. Incredulous
8. Inquisitive
9. Impressed

10. Mystified

11. Passionate

12. Playful

13. Replenished

14. Splendid

15. Shocked

16. Stunned

OBJECTIVE C: SMART ENGAGEMENT TO SUPPORT YOUTH IN IDENTIFYING NEEDS AND GETTING NEEDS MET APPROPRIATELY

We all know that strong emotions gone unchecked can cause us to act ridiculous or sabotage us in getting what we really want or need out of a situation. We also know that self-regulation prevents these disasters. Stopping to observe our feelings long enough to choose a word that accurately describes our feelings, then describing where in our bodies we feel the feeling, connects us to reasoning skills.

Strategies for Achieving Objective C: Getting Needs Met

After identifying the feeling word, and where the feeling is living in the body, encourage young people to ask themselves:

• "Why am I *(e.g., angry, sad, disappointed, frustrated, etc.)*? What is my (e.g., anger, sadness, disappointment, frustration, etc.) informing me of? What do I need? What is the best way to get my need met?

- Encourage young people to consider the different actions or inaction they can choose to get their need met.

  - **Note:** remind young people that this step about what they can do, not what others should do. In other words, "I need respect, so Susie needs to apologize to me for her rude behavior." This is not about Susie you do not want your emotional well-being dependent on her. Better to say, "I expect (need) my friends to respect my boundaries. Your behavior in the future will let me know whether you consider us friends."

These techniques will seem weird and odd when you and your young person begin this new process. We have not been taught these skills. We tend to use limited vocabulary to describe our emotions. We have not been taught how to connect emotions with needs or the importance of doing so. But we are human beings with six senses, the sixth sense is our emotional sense or compass. Our emotional health and overall well-being become remarkably improved when we pay attention to our sixth sense, the same way we pay attention to our other senses.

We would not stay in a room in which fumes were burning our eyes. We would not eat a plate of hot food as it burned our tongues. We are quick to leave environments or people who smell bad after our sense of smell alerts us, we feel uncomfortable and move to get our need (escape the smell) met. We cover our ears when a loud noise occurs. Why do we allow ourselves to feel so bad for such long time periods and refuse to act to feel better? It's because we haven't been taught how to use our emotions efficiently and effectively. Consequently, we establish patterns of "waiting" before we walk into the unknown called change—which tends to elicit fear.

Expand Youth's Needs-Based Vocabulary

Needs-based vocabulary includes words that describe the tangible (e.g., shelter, food) and intangible (e.g., love, respect, and understanding) needs of an individual.

Benefits of Using Needs-Based Vocabulary

To have a need met or satisfied, we must be able to identify the need. No one knows what you need better than you do! Below are behaviors to support you and your youth in developing a habit of using need words.

Strategies for Expanding Needs-Based Vocabulary

- Expand need-based vocabulary for you and your youth by posting a list of need words in places around your house (bathroom mirror, refrigerator etc.).

- Encourage youth to use words to describe their needs.

- Set a good example for youth by using needs words to identify your own needs.

Ten Categories of Human Needs

Category 1: Autonomy

1. **Elements of autonomy**
2. Choice
3. Freedom
4. Independence
5. Individuality
6. Self-empowerment
7. Solitude

Category 2: Nurturance

1. **Elements of nurturance**
2. Bonding
3. Caring
4. Nurturing
5. Physical affection
6. Warmth

Category 3: Mental Needs

1. **Elements of mental needs**
2. Awareness, consciousness
3. Comprehension
4. Discrimination
5. Information financial security
6. Reflection, analyzing, thinking
7. Stimulation
8. Understanding, clarity

Category 4 : Integrity

1. **Elements of integrity**
2. Authenticity
3. Dreams
4. Honesty
5. Purpose
6. Self-respect
7. Self-worth
8. Values
9. Vision

Category 5: Physical Survival

1. **Elements needed for physical survival**
2. Air
3. Food
4. Protection
5. Rest
6. Safety
7. Sex
8. Shelter
9. Water

Category 6: Self-Expression

1. **Elements needed for self-expression**
2. Creativity
3. Healing
4. Goals
5. Growth

6. Mastery
7. Meaning
8. Teaching

Category 7: Spiritual Energy

1. **Elements of spiritual energy**
2. Beauty
3. Aesthetic
4. Beingness (a state of spiritual being)
5. Communion
6. Harmony
7. Peace
8. Order—grace
9. Ritualize the sacred

Category 8: Relationships

1. **Elements of relationships**
2. Freedom to Choose
3. Honor
4. Respect
5. Security of family
6. Security of home
7. True love

Category 9: Celebrating life

1. **Elements of celebration of life**
2. Exercise, movement
3. Mourning of loss

4. Mourning of moments
5. Passion, intensity
6. Play, humor
7. Pleasure, delight
8. Stimulation, excitement

Category 10: Social-Emotional Independence

1. **Elements of social-emotional independence**
2. Acknowledgment, recognition, validation
3. Appreciation, admiration
4. Being heard, understanding
5. Community. family
6. Connection, communication, closeness
7. Contribution, giving, serving
8. Emotional safety, emotional freedom, relaxation
9. Equality, tolerance, justice
10. Friendship, companionship, sharing, intimacy
11. Love, affection, acceptance, being liked
12. Respect, fairness, consideration
13. Support, cooperation, empathy
14. Trust, reassurance, certainty

Using Real Life Experiences to Support Young People in Understanding the Connection Between Feelings and Needs

When young people express emotions, no matter the volume, they have a need that is urgent to them.

- A tantrum (no matter the age) is an expression of five to seven needs not met, mostly focused on *choice and being heard.*

- Frustration and disappointment tell us that a need hasn't been met. Just ask yourself... Why would you experience an emotion if you didn't have a need?

We help young people distinguish feelings from needs by providing them with practice opportunities to identify feelings and needs related to feeling. By providing young people with opportunities to practice *identifying* feelings and needs, we help them learn to distinguish feelings from needs.

Benefits of Identifying Feelings and Needs Related to Feelings in Real Life Situations

- The ability to identify a feeling and the need attached to it is a first step in building self-regulation.

- When we identify a need, we take the first step towards getting it satisfied.

The ideal time to help a young person identify their feelings and needs is when you catch them experiencing an emotion. Review the example situation below:

Situation: Your teen comes home from school acting angry.

Adult: "You seem upset."

Youth: "Yes, I'm furious. Laura borrowed my top last week, and without asking, she lent it to Barbara."

Adult: "It sounds like you need something. What do you think it is?"

Youth: "I think I need my top returned right now!"

Adult: "Are you furious because you don't have your top, or are you furious because Laura lent it out without your permission?"

Notice: this adult is encouraging the teen to really explore the need behind the emotion).

Youth: "I'm mad that Barbara has my top, and I'm mad that Laura lent it to her without my permission."

Adult: "I think you are saying that you feel angry that Barbara has your top and you need to get it back from her immediately. It also sounds like you're angry with Laura for lending it to Barbara because you need her to have respect for your personal items."

Youth: "Yes!"

Adult: "I understand why you are angry. What can you do to get your needs met?"

Youth: "I need to get my top back from Barbara and talk with Laura about respecting my things or I'm not lending them to her anymore."

Adult: "Sounds like you have a good plan to meet your needs."

Tip: The adult's goal is to lead the conversation in ways that help the young identify a feeling and the unmet need or needs attached to that feeling. By helping youth get these needs met, you empower them. For example, in the above situation, the youth can be proactive by retrieving her top. She doesn't need to wait for it to be returned. She can also set an appropriate boundary for the next time Laura borrows something from her.

The end goal is to assist youth in developing the sentence structure, "I'm feeling _____ because I need _____, and therefore I will _____ (to get my need met)."

It is perfectly acceptable for you to help by summarizing a teen's feelings and needs. However, you should wait until you have enough information to make an educated guess as to what the teen's feelings and needs are. No one likes to be told what they're feeling or what they need. But everyone likes to hear that they've been understood. With practice, youth will become very skilled at identifying their feelings and needs and at taking steps to have those needs met.

Using Stories and Movies to Support Young People in Understanding the Connection Between Feelings and Needs

Building a skill takes practice, but it also takes emotional context, and stories are an excellent way to provide this. With younger age groups, you can use any story that elicits a thoughtful discussion about feelings and needs. You can even buy fiction books to accomplish this task, or you can make up short stories. You can also rent movies, or buy movies, or check them out at the library. This way, you can use these movies or stories as teaching tools for helping your young person identify emotions and needs.

For example, let's assume you and your young person are reading or watching a story about a boy named Nathan. It is Nathan's first day at a new school. He's eleven years old, and in sixth grade. He gets up out of his seat to sharpen his pencil. While walking down the aisle, a student named William sticks his leg out, and Nathan trips over it and falls. The other students in the class burst out into laughter. No one helps Nathan get to his feet. The teacher remains silent.

Here are some questions you might use to turn this story into a learning experience for your young person:

- "How do you think Nathan felt when he tripped? What do you think he needed?"

- "Why do you think William stuck his leg out into the aisle? What do you think he needed?"

- "Why do you think the students laughed when Nathan tripped? What do you think the students needed?"

- "Why do you think the teacher remained silent? What do you think she needed?"

Reminders for Young People

- We can't control others, but we can control our response to others.

- We can't control all situations, but we can control our responses to situations.

- We can express feelings and uncomfortable thoughts with a trusted caregiver.

- We can observe our own thoughts and feelings and explore how to cope with stressful or complex situations.

- It's important to consider the outcome of our actions before we act. This way, we can avoid unwanted outcomes.

- We can change our thinking or how we think about a situation!

- It is important to remain solution-oriented when we face challenges. This way, we can address the challenge in ways that will benefit us.

- When a mistake is made, no matter how big or small, we put it into the past as quickly as we can. But, we also do this in a way that keeps us accountable for our actions (e.g., making honest reconciliation when we've hurt someone).

Strategy 11: The Identity Platform

How to Help Your Young Person Find their Purpose and Place in the World

Identity

Identity is the sum of our qualities, values, beliefs, and characteristics.

Platform

A platform is a plan, a design, or something to stand on. Therefore, the identity platform is the values, beliefs, and characteristics we stand on to navigate our lives.

The Identity Platform

The identity platform is a strategy that helps youth discover their values, beliefs, and characteristics by asking them to respond to three questions:

1. Who am I?"
2. "What is my purpose?"
3. "Where do I belong?"

These are considered pivotal questions because the answers drive our daily thinking, decisions, and behaviors. The answers to these questions provide a roadmap for a life driven by intention. It gives a young person a firm foundation to stand on when everything around them seems to be pushing them in different directions.

Adults who provide young people with the strategies to explore, discover, and recognize their identity are giving young people a magical formula that can be reused throughout their entire life. Our identities, purpose, and sense of belonging often change as a result of biological development, new experiences, and new discoveries about ourselves, others, and the world. Youth need strategies for staying in touch with who they are and what they stand for so that they can continue to lead productive, meaningful, and joyful lives.

Case in point, I was a college professor for fifteen years. I knew with complete certainty that my position reflected my identity, purpose, and sense of belonging. But I also knew when it was time to move on. Deep within me I wanted to do more for young people than what was possible in my college faculty position. I also recognized that while working at the college, I had been preparing myself and building the foundation (experience, research, talents, drive, relationships, etc.) for moving into my new purpose.

The greatest gift we can give young people is to support them in discovering who they were truly born to be—who they *deserve* to be. It's also important to give them strategies for checking in with themselves as they go through life's changes.

Rarely are youth given the opportunities to stop, think about, and choose virtues to live by. Rarely are youth shown how to use their chosen virtues to think, decide, and behave with integrity. Consequently, too many youths are unable to realize the personal empowerment that comes with being true to oneself. Therefore, the objectives of the identity platform are to give youth opportunities for self-discovery and being the master of their life journey.

Benefits of Using the Identity Platform

In almost every environment—whether at home, educational institutions, extracurricular activities, or places of employment—young people are bombarded with expectations, rules, and policies. Everyday youth are bombarded with messages from the media, peers, and technology telling them who they should be, how they should act, what they should wear, who they should and shouldn't talk to, what they should or shouldn't eat, what's cool what isn't cool, what looks good, what looks bad, what they need, what they don't need, etc. All this noise makes it difficult for a young person to hear their own voice. Supporting youth in developing a roadmap for the kind of life they see as exciting helps them listen to their own voice. *The Identify Platform* provides youth with practical strategies to use in everyday life, which helps them operate above the noise.

Objectives

A. Support youth in exploring the question: "Who am I?"

B. Support youth in exploring the question: "What is my purpose?"

C. Support youth in exploring the question: "Where do I belong?"

OBJECTIVE A: SUPPORT YOUTH IN EXPLORING THE QUESTION: "WHO AM I?"

The Pivotal Question: "Who am I?"

Seeking to Discover: Identity

What Resonates Within:

- Virtues.

- What feeds my spirit?

- What moves me?

Benefits:

- You can be true to what you stand for.

- You like who you are!

The question, "Who am I?" tells us who we are at our core. It defines our authentic identity. Our basic values and beliefs about ourselves, others, and the world we live in are "baked" into this identity. Our identity—our beliefs, values, and virtues—drives our daily thinking, decisions, and behaviors and thus shapes our lives. So, by answering this question, we discover the driving force of our lives.

Benefits of Identity

We must know who we are before we can stand up for who we are.

Knowing who we are allows us to self-assert—a core communication skill that gives us the confidence to express thoughts, emotions, beliefs, and opinions effectively and honestly. This is how we stand up for ourselves, our beliefs, and our personal truths.

Strategies for Achieving Objective A

- Introduce youth to the "virtues inventory" under Objective C (below).

- Support youth in understanding the relationship between virtues and needs (e.g., our virtues allow us to meet our own needs and the needs of others, just as other people's virtues help them meet their needs and ours).

- Remind youth that when we implement a virtue we must temper it with consideration. In other words, honesty is good but without using consideration of how our honesty affects others, we may inadvertently use honesty in ways that are unkind and hurtful.

OBJECTIVE B: SUPPORT YOUTH IN EXPLORING THE QUESTION: 'WHAT IS MY PURPOSE?'

The Pivotal Question: "What is my purpose?"

Seeking to Discover: Meaning

What Resonates Within:

- Interests.
- Natural talents.
- Strengths.

Benefits:

- Clarity to plan and take steps to make your goals and dreams come true.

- Live the life you choose to live.

To discover our purpose is to find meaning in what we do. I speak with many adults who are unhappy with what they do in life. They complain that their work has no meaning to them. They literally can't stand going to work. In questioning them, I find that their work has nothing to do with their core values, their interests, or even their natural talents. This is a common and emotionally painful problem for adults, so imagine the difference you'll make by helping a young person solve it early in life.

To introduce youth to the concept of a purpose-driven life—a purpose-driven life is a meaningful and significant life.

Strategies for Achieving Objective B

- Observe youth to discover their natural inclinations, interests, preferences, and talents.

  - Preferences begin to reveal themselves early in life. Notice the types of activities youth are drawn to (e.g., caregivers, risk takers, high energy, fashion conscious, hair stylists, makeup artists, idea people, science or how things work, music, fact finder, leader, sports, communication, fairness, equity, baker, cooking, photography, clay work, home decoration, writer, researcher, entrepreneur, outdoors, water lover, animal caregiver, etc.).

- Expose youth to a wide variety of music, art, dance, and sports activities that they can observe, listen to, and participate in.

  - Giving youth a wide variety of experiences takes time but does not need to be costly. Use books, radio, computers, DVDs, CDs, and visits to local cultural festivals and specialty shops to offer unique opportunities and experiences to youth. Local libraries lend more than books; they lend movies too. Identify events that are advertised in local newspapers or on the radio.

  - Once you determine your youth is really interested in something, consider deepening their experience. For example, imagine your youth wants to watch a ballet movie over and over again. Perhaps you can find a college or performing arts school that performs locally at minimal cost.

- Follow your young person's interests and let them to take the lead. Be careful not to let your own bias get in the way.

- Create conditions that are safe for youth to express their interests.

- Create emotional safety when your young person makes mistakes.

  - Use healthy laughter to enjoy the experience of making a mistake and treat every mistake as a positive learning experience.

- Use various personality tools to encourage diverse thinking and acceptance of different approaches.

- Identify ways to serve self, family, and community.

- Encourage youth to keep an open mind. Our preferences, likes, and dislikes change as we age. An eleven-year-old may snub his nose at a classical tune you play for him, but at seventeen he may find it—and other classical music—calming.

- Cultivate a learning environment that allows youth to experience frustration. Frustration and irritation can anchor long-term learning in a healthy way, especially considering that some lessons can only be learned as a result of frustration.

- Encourage the journey to discover purpose by replacing "should" or "shouldn't" with statements that engage the imagination.

- For example, you need quiet, but your youth is singing louder that you would like in the house,

  - Rather than saying something negative, like, "You shouldn't sing so loud; it's disturbing me," you might try saying, "Would you be willing to lower your voice? It seems you enjoy singing. I just need some quiet right now."

Call attention to people with a purpose-driven life.

  - Read biographies of people who have lived (or who are living) a purpose-driven life.

  - Engage youth in conversations about their heroes or those they admire and ask, "What do you think their purpose is? How do you think their purpose drove them to be who they are today?"

OBJECTIVE C: SUPPORT YOUTH IN EXPLORING THE QUESTION: 'WHERE DO I BELONG? AM I SIGNIFICANT?'

The Pivotal Question: "Where do I belong?" "Am I a significant member of society?"

Seeking to Discover: Appreciation and being valued as a member of a family, a community, and society.

What Resonates Within: Feeling, knowing, believing you are accepted by others.

To discover where we belong is to discover where we are appreciated and valued. When we walk into a place—whether home, school, job, or some other location for enjoyment or an experience—we immediately feel comfortable or uncomfortable. The feeling of comfort comes from the innate feeling that we are where we belong. On the other hand, our discomfort might be an indicator that we are *not* in a place where we belong.

Perhaps we are shy or uncomfortable in a new place or when having first-time experiences. However, if we continue to feel odd, uncomfortable, undervalued or unappreciated after being in a situation or place several times, that's a sign that we're in a place or situation where we don't belong.

We all know when we "belong." The place or situation feels warm, friendly, and inviting. We know what it is like to enter a room when everyone is laughing, and enjoying each other, or they're interacting for a common purpose or goal. But, do we fit in? Do we belong? Most of us intuitively know this! But it's important to pay attention to our intuition and make sure we don't try to adjust to a place or a situation where we simply don't belong. Youth need to be reminded, "When a situation or person makes you feel uncomfortable, it is okay to excuse yourself and walk away." Yes, it takes courage, but living life in integrity takes courage not conformity. Conformity is easy but the cost might be more than one wants to pay.

Benefits of Belonging/Significance

- We feel appreciated and valued as an individual member of society.

- We cope better with challenging situations.

- We have a support system.

- Knowing we are a significant member of society inspires us.

Strategies for Achieving Objective C

- Encourage youth to use core values as a meter to determine where they do or don't belong.

- Core values can help a young person decide if they belong in a conversation with their peers. For example, youth who claim kindness as a virtue may not belong in a conversation where hurtful gossip is occurring.

- Encourage youth to think about their virtues during different situations and to use them to act (e.g., walk away, speak up, ask for help, etc.).

Virtues Inventory

A

Acceptance—The act of accepting something or someone. **Complements:** Contentment, forgiveness. **Transcends:** Denial, rejection

Assertiveness—Disposed to or characterized by bold or confident statements and behavior. **Complements:** Confidence, courage. **Transcends:** Self-doubt, shyness

Authenticity—True to one's own personality, spirit, or character. **Complements:** Honesty, integrity. **Transcends:** Low Self-esteem

B

Beauty—The qualities in a person or a thing that give pleasure to the senses or the mind. **Complements:** Joyfulness, peace. **Transcends:** Ugliness.

C

Caring—Feeling or showing concern for other people. **Complements:** Compassion, kindness. **Transcends:** Cruelty, insensitivity.

Cleanliness—The practice of keeping yourself and your surroundings clean. **Complements:** Orderliness, purity. **Transcends:** Dirtiness.

Commitment—An agreement or pledge to do something in the future. Complements: Loyalty, perseverance. **Transcends:** Lack of direction.

Compassion—Sympathetic consciousness of others' distress together with a desire to alleviate it. **Complements:** Caring, understanding. **Transcends:** Grief, judgment

Confidence—A feeling or belief that you can do something well or succeed at something. **Complements:** Assertiveness, courage. **Transcends:** Self-doubt, uncertainty.

Consideration—The act of thinking carefully about something you will make a decision about. **Complements:** Caring, compassion. **Transcends:** Selfishness.

Contentment—The state of being happy and satisfied. **Complements:** Fulfillment, joy. **Transcends:** Dissatisfaction, restlessness.

Cooperation—A situation in which people work together to do something. **Complements:** Teamwork, unity. **Transcends:** Defiance.

Courage—Mental or moral strength to venture, persevere, and withstand danger, fear, or difficulty. **Complements:** Boldness, confidence. **Transcends:** Fear, self-doubt.

Creativity—The ability to make new things or think of new ideas. **Complements:** Joy, purposefulness. **Transcends:** Ordinary.

D

Detachment—Lack of emotion or of personal interest. **Complements:** Faith, freedom. **Transcends:** Control.

Determination—A quality that makes you continue trying to do or achieve something that is difficult. **Complements:** Commitment, tenaciousness. Transcends: Complacency.

Dignity—A way of appearing or behaving that suggests seriousness and self-control. **Complements:** Honor, respect. **Transcends:** Egoism, selfishness.

E

Encouragement—Something that makes someone more determined, hopeful, or confident. **Complements:** Support, caring. **Transcends:** Self-doubt, discouragement.

Enthusiasm — Strong excitement about something. A strong feeling of active interest in something liked or enjoyed. **Complements:** Energy, motivation. **Transcends:** Boredom, indifference.

Ethical—Following accepted rules of behavior. Using morally right and good behavior. **Complements:** Fairness, respect. **Transcends:** Immorality

Excellence—Extremely high quality. **Complements:** Dignity, honor, integrity, respect. **Transcends:** Mediocrity.

F

Fairness—Treating people in a way that does not favor some over others. **Complements:** Equality, justice. **Transcends:** Grievance, injustice,

Faith—Strong belief or trust in someone or something. **Complements:** Confidence, hope, trust. **Transcends:** Apprehension, doubt.

Flexibility—Willing to change or to try different things. **Complements:** Detachment, understanding. **Transcends:** Stubbornness.

Forgiveness—The act of forgiving someone or something. **Complements:** Freedom, peace. **Transcends:** Anger, bitterness.

Friendliness—Acting like a friend; kind and helpful. **Complements:** Kindness, tact. **Transcends:** Shyness.

G

Generosity—The quality of being kind, understanding, and not selfish; the quality of being generous. **Complements:** Kindness, service. **Transcends:** Stinginess, self-centeredness.

Gentleness—Having or showing a kind and quiet nature; not harsh or violent. **Complements:** Patience, peace. **Transcends:** Aggression.

Graciousness—Very polite in a way that shows respect. **Complements:** Dignity, tact. **Transcends:** Disrespect, rudeness.

Gratitude—A feeling of appreciation or thanks. **Complements:** Hope, joy, peace. **Transcends:** Disappointment, pain.

H

Harmonious—Having parts that are related or combined in a pleasing way. **Complements:** Unity. **Transcends:** Hostility.

Helpfulness—Making it easier to do a job. Deal with a problem. Giving assistance. **Complements:** Graciousness, service to assist. **Transcends:** Negativity.

Honesty—The quality of being fair and truthful. **Complements:** Integrity, truthfulness. **Transcends:** Deceitfulness

Honor — Respect that is given to someone who is admired. **Complements:** Dignity, respect. **Transcends:** Shame.

Hope—To want something to happen. To think that it could happen. To think something could be true. **Complements:** Faith, joy, trust. **Transcends:** Despair, frustration.

Humility—The quality or state of not thinking you are better than other people. **Complements:** Modesty. **Transcends:** Arrogance, pride.

I

Idealism—The attitude of a person who believes that it is possible to live according to very high standards of behavior and honesty. **Complements:** Confidence, hope. **Transcends:** Cynicism, pessimism.

Integrity—The quality of being honest and fair. **Complements:** Honesty, trust. **Transcends:** Corruption, deceitfulness.

Imaginative—Having or showing an ability to think of new and interesting ideas; having or showing imagination.

Complements: Creativity. **Transcends:** Ordinary, rationalism.

J

Joyfulness—Filled with joy. Feeling, causing, or showing great happiness. **Complements:** Hope, peace, love. **Transcends:** Discontent, suffering.

Justice—The process or result of using laws to fairly judge and punish crimes and criminals. **Complements:** Fairness, integrity. **Transcends:** Discrimination

K

Kindness—A kind act. The quality or state of being kind. **Complements:** Caring, compassionate. **Transcends:** Cruelty, loneliness.

L

Love—A feeling of strong or constant affection for a person. **Complements:** Caring, forgiveness, unity. **Transcends:** Fear.

Loyalty—The quality of being loyal to someone or something. **Complements:** Honesty, true. **Transcends:** Betrayal.

M

Moderation—The avoidance of excess or extremes. **Complements:** Diligence, responsibility. **Transcends:** Obsessions, overindulgence.

Modestly—The quality or state of being unassuming or moderate in the estimation of one's abilities. **Complements:** Humility. **Transcends:** Self-importance.

O

Optimistic—Having or showing hope for the future. Expecting good things to happen. **Complements:** Hope, joyfulness **Transcends:** Pessimism.

Orderliness — Arranged or organized in a logical way. **Complements:** Cleanliness, purity. **Transcends:** Chaos.

P

Passionate—Having, showing, or expressing strong emotions or strong beliefs. **Complements:** Enthusiasm, purposefulness. **Transcends:** Indifference.

Patience—The skill to wait without becoming upset. **Complements:** Determination, calm. **Transcends:** Frustration.

Peace—A state of tranquility or quiet. **Complements:** Love, serenity, unity. **Transcends:** Anger, cruelty.

Perseverance—Despite challenges, sustained effort to accomplish a goal or task. *Complements:* Commitment, determination, resilience. *Transcends:* Laziness.

Preparedness—The state or quality of being ready. **Complements:** Excellence, orderliness. **Transcends:** Complacency

Purposefulness—Having a purpose as in something set up as an object or end to be attained. **Complements:** Creativity, commitment, joyfulness. **Transcends:** Boredom, indifference.

R

Reliability—The quality of being trustworthy or of performing consistently well. **Complements:** Integrity, loyalty. **Transcends:** Untrustworthiness.

Respect—A feeling of deep admiration for someone or something elicited by their abilities, qualities, or achievements. **Complements:** Dignity, reverence. **Transcends:** Inconsideration.

Responsibility—The state or fact of having a duty to deal with something or of having control over someone. **Complements:** Courtesy, tact, trust. **Transcends:** Selfishness.

Reverence—Deep respect for someone or something. **Complements:** Respect, worth. **Transcends:** Hatred.

S

Self-discipline—The ability you have to control and motivate yourself, stay on track, and do what is right.

Complements: Commitment, determination. **Transcends:** Chaos, unruliness

Service—The action of helping or doing work for someone. **Complements:** Compassion, generosity, purposefulness. **Transcends:** Lack of concern, self-centeredness.

Sincerity—The quality of being free from pretense, deceit, or hypocrisy. **Complements:** Authentic. **Transcends:** Disingenuousness

T

Tact—Sensitivity in dealing with others or with difficult issues. **Complements:** Graciousness, responsibility. **Transcends:** Clumsiness.

Temperate—Showing moderation or self-restraint. **Complements:** Moderation. **Transcends:** Excessiveness.

Tenacious—Not readily relinquishing a position, principle, or course of action; determined. **Complements:** Perseverance. **Transcends:** Indecision

Thankfulness — Someone feeling or showing gratitude. **Complements:** Gratitude, thoughtfulness. **Transcends:** Unappreciative.

Tolerance—The ability or willingness to tolerate something, in particular the existence of opinions or behavior that one does not necessarily agree with. **Complements:** Patience, tenacious. **Transcends:** Narrow-mindedness.

Trust—Firm belief in the reliability, truth, ability, or strength of someone or something. **Complements:** Loyalty, respect. **Transcends:** Doubt, skepticism.

Truthfulness—Telling or disposed to tell the truth. **Complements:** Honesty, faith, trust. **Transcends:** Corruption, deceit.

U

Understanding—The ability to understand something, comprehension. **Complements:** Kindness, tolerance. **Transcends:** Egoism.

Unity—The state of being united or joined as a whole. **Complements:** Harmony, love, peace. **Transcends:** Loneliness.

V

Visionary—Thinking about or planning the future with imagination or wisdom. **Complements:** Imagination, leadership. **Transcends:** Lack of inspiration.

W

Wisdom—The quality of having experience, knowledge, and good judgment. The quality of being wise. **Complements:** Idealism, visionary. **Transcends:** Lack of intelligence.

Wonder—A feeling of surprise mingled with admiration, caused by something beautiful, unexpected, unfamiliar, or inexplicable. **Complements:** Imagination, creative. **Transcends:** Boredom.

Virtues for Life, https://www.virtuesforlife.com/virtues-list/

STRATEGY 12: APPROPRIATE COMMUNICATION

HOW TO CUSTOMIZE YOUR COMMUNICATION FOR YOUR YOUNG PERSON'S AGE AND ABILITY LEVEL

Words can trigger emotions. They create a wide variety of feelings, both for those who speak them, and those who hear them. It is important for caregivers to recognize that youth require different communication strategies, depending on their age and their level of development. Below are communication strategies for all ages.

For age-specific strategies, see Reference Module B: "Age Appropriate Communication Strategies."

COMMUNICATION STRATEGIES FOR ALL AGES

- Choose time-ins (rather than time-outs) to help young people discover and practice appropriate responses to situations.

- Use positive tone and body language.

- Create safe opportunities for youth to express their feelings. For example, if a young person appears angry, rather than saying, "Stop yelling and crying," you might say, "I want to understand you. What can you do to calm yourself? I want to help."

Tip: The child who has been working on calming strategies, such as slow breaths, will be able to respond to a question such as, "What can you do to calm yourself?" The adolescent who has received "Smart Engagement Strategy 10" training will also be able to engage in calming strategies using feeling and need based vocabulary words.

THE CHILD DEVELOPMENT INSTITUTE SUGGESTS THE FOLLOWING GUIDELINES FOR PARENT-CHILD COMMUNICATION

The points below were retrieved from Shushan Khachatryan (http://www.shushantherapy.com /communication-problems/ basic-principles-of-good-parentchild-communication/).

- Demonstrate genuine interest in youth's endeavors. Offer your assistance if necessary.

- When youth want to have a conversation, then give them your full attention (e.g., put the cell phone down, turn off the television, turn off the radio, set the computer aside).

- Provide privacy. *Don't* include others who are not specifically meant to be included when speaking to youth.

- When necessary, sit or kneel so you can make eye contact with youth you are conversing with rather than towering over them.

- Anger thwarts objectivity. Never attempt communication when you are angry.

- Try to be rested, rather than tired, before any communication endeavors with youth.

- Listen patiently with polite body language and using respectful oral language.

- Ask youth "What happened?" rather than, "Why did you do that?"

- It is smart to share your knowledge of a situation with youth. Let them know what you've been told.

- Adult talking should be kept at a minimum.

- Suggest or help youth identify some solutions and help them with the steps to solve a problem.

- Emphasize your acceptance of youth regardless of their missteps.

- Use encouragement for youth's communication endeavors.

Resist the urge to:
- Interrupt young people when they are trying to tell their story.

- Preach or put a moral spin on everything a young person says. This closes the door to communication. Youth will shut down. The goal is to keep communication open.

- Embarrass youth or put him or her on the spot in front of others. This will likely lead to resentment and hostility, not good communication.

- Text or answer your phone during your conversation with a young person.

- Use discouraging words such as *dumb, stupid,* or *lazy* or statements such as "Are you stupid? What you are doing makes no sense!" or "You could improve your grades if you weren't so lazy!"

- Interrupt the young person as they tell you a story, thus not allowing their own theme to develop. This is the parent who reacts to the incidentals of a message while the main idea is lost. For example, the child starts to share what happened with friends, but the parent interrupts. "I don't care what they're doing, but you had better not be involved in anything that breaks our family rules."

PART B: THE POSITIVE YOUTH GUIDANCE SYSTEM

FIVE STRATEGIES TO HELP YOUTH OF STRESS AND TRAUMA

Youth who have experienced chronic trauma or excessive stress— particularly in their formative years when attachment and brain structure are being built—will have unique challenges. For these young people, you will need strategies which encourage solid, foundational thinking skills. These strategies will promote self-trust, relationship trust, empathy, and self-regulation.

STRATEGY 1: THE MAGIC OF ASKING

HOW TO HELP AT-RISK YOUTH DEVELOP CAUSAL THINKING

- *Routines* provide youth with a sense of order and predictability. This allows them to understand that the world has some consistency and that there are rules and guidelines. This encourages "if-then/cause and effect" thinking, which is pivotal for decision-making throughout life.

- *Curiosity questions* help youth learn to come up with their own answers. You do this by asking instead of telling.

EXAMPLES OF THE DIFFERENCE BETWEEN ASKING AND TELLING

1. **Asking:** "How will you stay warm outside?" **Telling:** "Put on your jacket."

2. **Asking:** "What needs to happen before bath time?" **Telling:** "Pick up the toys before bath time."

3. **Asking:** "What happened? How did it happen? What were you trying to accomplish? What might you do differently next time?" **Telling:** "The next time you need to ask me to do it for you!"

- *Provide choices* whenever possible:

  - You can have an orange or a banana. You choose.

  - You can do your homework now or in an hour. You choose.

  - You can do your chores and go out this evening or ignore your chores and stay home. You choose.

- *Practice play,* including outside games and board games. Make sure youth experience a beginning, middle, and end. This will teach them that routines are predictable and structured.

STRATEGY 2: THE MAGIC OF TRUST

HOW TO BUILD AND SUPPORT TRUST WITH AT-RISK YOUTH

- Maintain routines, predictability and consistency.

- Plan ahead and let youth know in advance when a change is necessary. For example, "Wednesday we were going to the pool, but it will be shut down. I am open to choosing something else to do, what about you?"

- Allow time for youth to get ready or adjust. For example, "In ten minutes we will be getting in the car, so you have five minutes to say your good-byes."

- Relationships must be based on respect and dignity. Remember that adults and youth have intellectual, creative, emotional, social, and physical needs that are typically not in sync. Both are important. The response to a young person's needs are critical.

  - For example, your teen wants to go to a party. He has a need to socialize. As a parent or caregiver, you have the emotional need for him to be safe. Rather than say "you cannot go to the party because I don't know your friend's parents and it's my job to keep you safe," you might say, "I understand that a party with friends is fun. How can I meet Jim's parents to get more information? I need to know you will be in a safe place."

The latter statement reveals respect for the needs of both you and the teen.

- Allow youth to contribute in meaningful ways (chores, meal preparation, choosing healthy meals, gardening, laundry, feeding the family pet, etc.).

STRATEGY 3: THE MAGIC OF BUILDING CONSCIENCE

HOW TO HELP AT-RISK YOUTH DEVELOP CONSCIENCE

- Listen to youth's stories without judgment. Use reflective listening to explore and respond to the emotions under the "stuff" (e.g., "Sounds like you felt really angry/sad/excited.").

- Provide opportunities for developing relationships with others. Use curiosity questions to talk about these relationships (e.g., "Why did you choose her to be your friend?" or "What do you like about him?").

- Observe safety needs. Remove youth from overstimulating environments or step in to assist them in coping if you catch them getting agitated.

- Treat mistakes as learning opportunities or problem-solving opportunities—*not* as a reason to punish. Help youth come up with solutions.

- Use all the strategies in Part A of the Positive Youth Guidance System.

Strategy 4: The Magic of Self-Regulation

How to Help At-Risk Youth Build Self-Regulation

One of the most important things we can provide for those who have been through chronic trauma is tools for self-management and/or self-regulation. Here are some things to start with:

- Teach the young person the "brain in the palm model" from chapter 15 (see bonus chapters). Young people who have a visual model of "flipping their lid," will recognize when they're becoming dysregulated.

- Discuss and encourage the young person to find and use a safe space—a place to chill out when they notice they're becoming dysregulated. They can use a corner of their room, space under the stairs, or a favorite chair. When they have flipped their lid, we can invite them to go there. For example, "You are really mad right now. Would it help for you to spend a few minutes in your chill-out space? Or would you like to sit with me until you feel better? You choose."

Use mindfulness or mindfulness-based strategies. Here are some examples from Goldie Hawn's book *Mind Up*:

- Have young person close eyes and concentrate on sounds they can hear inside the room where they're for one to two minutes, and then see if they can hear sounds outside the room for one to two minutes.

- Use Chinese chimes, a prayer bowl, or anything with a slowly decreasing sound. Have the young person close his or her eyes, ring the chime, and open his or her eyes when he or she no longer can hear the sound.

- Encourage the young person to sit down and breathe for a few minutes each day—paying attention to breathing in and out through the nose. Use a Hoberman sphere during this breathing session. The young person holds the sphere and using their fingers to expand it outward, as they breath in, and then collapses it, as they breath out.

- Gather some household items that make noise (spoon and pan, pencil to tap on a surface, paper to crinkle up). Have the young person close his or her eyes and focus on the sound you are about to make. Make a noise with one of the objects. Ask young person some questions about the experience. For example, "How did you feel when that happened?" or "Could you hear better with your eyes closed? What kind of sound did that make?"

- Gather a few objects that look very similar—several rocks or leaves. Have the young person take one and spend a few minutes looking at it, really getting to know it. Then put it in a bag or box, mix with other like objects, and see if the young person can pick the one that was theirs. Ask them, "Was this hard/easy? Why?"

- Sit outside with young person. Encourage the young person to close his or her eyes (you too!) and spend a few minutes listening to all the sounds he or she is aware of.

- Invite the young person to lie on his or her back on the grass (or on a blanket) outside or in a park and spend a few minutes discussing with him or her what he or she can see from this position.

- Encourage the young person to do one daily activity, mindfully. For example, while brushing their teeth have them pay attention to each tooth as they brush, to the feel of the toothbrush on that tooth, to the taste of the toothpaste, and to the smoothness of the tooth after it has been brushed.

- Have the young person lie on his or her back with legs straight. Take one or two deep breaths. Ask the young person to slowly bring his or her knees to his or her chest and hug his or her legs. Breathe. Have the young person notice any soreness in his or her body. Slowly let his or her legs drop to one side. Breathe. Then move legs to the young person's other side. Breathe. Have him or her bring his or her legs to center and slowly allow him or her to return to extended position. Breathe.

- Practice *brain gym* activities. Dr. Paul Dennison wrote *Simple Activities for Whole Brain Learning.* There are also a wide variety of brain gym or brain exercises demonstrated on YouTube videos. These are physical exercises that promote the connections in the brain and are excellent strategies to do with youth and to encourage them to do themselves. They're all helpful in assisting youth to self-regulate.

STRATEGY 5: THE MAGIC OF THE ABCD METHOD

HOW TO HELP AT-RISK YOUTH BECOME GOOD COMMUNICATORS

I suggest using the ABCD Method to model positive communication and problem-solving skills. This method will also help your young person practice and hone their own positive communication skills. It's also a great way to implement bidirectional good communication *and* appreciative inquiry while building critical thinking skills, positive self-image, self-regulation, self-control, confidence, and mutual respect between you and your young person.

This method can be used with young children, preteens, teens, and young adults. It is great for empowering young people to learn appropriate intellectual, creative, emotional, social, and physical behaviors. It also supports young people in being successful with a wide variety of tasks. Most importantly, it will help them learn to live by their values and to be true to their word.

Parents and other caregivers open-up bidirectional good communication by appreciative inquiry. This is the fundamental idea behind the ABCD model. The ABCD Method can be used before or after inappropriate behavior occurs. For example, we can stop a young child from running into the street and immediately engage the ABCD method, or we can use the ABCD method after a child runs into the street. The same is true when working with adolescents and young adults. We can use the ABCD Method to discuss issues that might prevent the teen from getting home by curfew or we can use the ABCD method after the teen arrives home after curfew.

- **Antecedents:** Identify the thing or things which could cause or has caused a young person's inappropriate behavior.

- **Behavior:** Identify the behavior that could result from the antecedent or that has occurred because of the antecedent.

- **Consequence:** Identify the potential consequences or the consequences of the behavior.

- **Dialogue:** Discuss all three of the above with your young person. The goal of dialogue is to help young people self-regulate, prepare, think in terms of long-term effects of their behaviors; and ways to protect themselves from using behaviors that could result in an unwanted consequence.

EXAMPLE SITUATIONS USING THE ABCD METHOD

Example Situation 1: You and your friends are sitting in your front yard, and your children are playing together. The children are all between four and six years old. You notice your five-year-old is heading to the street to retrieve the ball the children are playing with. You jump up and stop her immediately, then engage the ABCD Method (prior to the child going into the street) as demonstrated in the diagram below:

IDENTIFY **ANTECEDENTS:**	IDENTIFY **BEHAVIOR:**
• **WHAT** DO YOU SEE IN THE STREET THAT MAKES IT UNSAFE? • **WHAT** WOULD HAPPEN IF YOU RAN INTO THE STREET WITH ALL THOSE CARS?	• **RUNNING** INTO THE STREET BEFORE CHECKING FOR CARS AND MAKING SURE IT IS SAFE.
DIALOGUE WITH **CHILD:**	IDENTIFY **CONSEQUENCE:**
• "**WHAT** CAN YOU DO THE NEXT TIME YOUR BALL ROLLS INTO THE STREET?" • "**LET'S** STAND HERE, AND YOU TELL ME WHEN IT'S SAFE TO GO INTO THE STREET." • "**WHAT** CAN YOU DO IF YOU AREN'T SURE WHEN IT IS SAFE?"	• "**YOU** COULD GET HURT" • "**DADDY** WOULD BE SAD." • "**YOU** COULDN'T PLAY WITH YOUR FRIENDS FOR A LONG TIME." • "**YOU** WOULD GET HURT."

Example Situation 2: Your teenager is supposed to be home no later than midnight. It is 12:45 a.m., and you are worried. You've called them three times, but keep getting their voice mail. You've left three urgent messages telling them you are concerned and that they need to call home immediately.

Fast forward to 1:05 a.m. Your teen walks in the door. Now that you aren't at your wit's end worried sick about, you calmly start a dialogue with them:

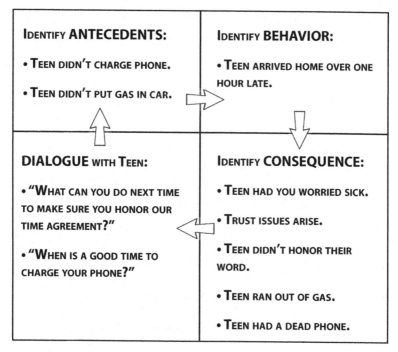

You: "Why are you late?"

Teen: "I ran out of gas."

You: "Why didn't you answer your phone or call me?"

Teen: "I tried, but my phone was dead."

Notice that in this example, the behavior has already happened. This will slightly change how you apply the ABCD model:

The ABCD method is an excellent way to explore and discuss possible situations that young people might find themselves in. Adults can help young people think about different types of antecedents, behaviors, and consequences of situations before a situation occurs. When adults do this, they help youth practice self-regulation which is needed to keep youth safe as they mature and are given more freedom.

For example, your sixteen-year-old has been invited to a birthday party. What are some of the natural concerns you have? Will an adult be present to chaperone? Will alcohol or drugs be at the party? What types of kids will be at the party? You might ask your young person questions like this to help identify potential antecedents:

- "What will you do if you feel unsafe at the party?"

- "What if you notice a friend is behaving unsafe?"

- "What if you notice illegal activities are going on?"

You can use each of these questions as antecedents to possible behaviors and consequences. This way, you can help your teen practice appropriate behaviors and responses. Remember to do this from the young person's perspective. Teens want to look cool, and they might worry that your responses will make them look "uncool." The ABCD method will help you listen, ask questions, and to use bidirectional good communication and appreciative inquiry in a way that promotes mutual respect. Teens can do the right thing and be viewed as "cool" for doing it. Telling a friend "I care about you, lets get you home" is much cooler than watching your friend shove a handful of unknown drugs into their mouth and drop dead or go into a coma. If anyone tells a teen that they are ruining the party for interceding on friend's behalf, our teens must recognize that the person saying that has no regard for others and must be ignored. In other words, "are you going to help your friend or listen to an idiot, what makes sense to you?"

Below is an example of using the ABCD method to help any young person succeed in various situations. With this model, you can explore antecedents, expected behaviors, possible outcomes, and have dialogue about specific issues. It will also help you address antecedents which might impede your young person's ability to navigate different types of situations appropriately and safely.

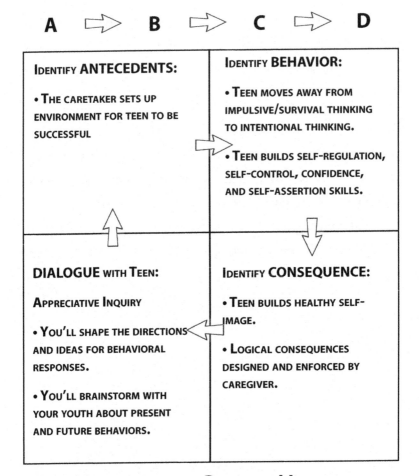

Need Help with the Positive Youth Guidance System?

Please visit xtraordinaryyouth.com to ask Dr. Kim a question, watch training videos, sign up for private coaching with Dr. Kim, or inquire about live or online workshops for organizations or individuals.

Chapter 10: ExtraOrdinary Youth and the Five Selves

Every organism has characteristics that are unique to its biology. These characteristics allow us to distinguish between the various life forms on our planet. Likewise, all human beings have defining characteristics, no matter what region, culture or time era they're born in.

In Chapter One, I introduced the concept of the five selves and the role they play in developing the *whole person*. I adopted this concept from work by Joanne Hendrick and Patricia Weismann who wrote the *Whole Child*. Their work discusses the five-selves as the: intellectual/cognitive, creative, emotional, social, and physical aspects that comprise the whole child. Their work is used to train early childhood educators by considering the needs and skills associated with each of the five selves. In my work, I emphasize that the five selves are universal to all humans, including adults. I did this to expand the early childhood education model to schools and homes of adolescents. Understanding the five selves is also a great way for adults to understand themselves and identify their own needs and skills—adults can ask themselves how their needs, skills, or lack of either affect their interactions and expectations of young people.

Consider that young people enter their homes and their classroom s with skills and needs that affect their behaviors. The best way to get another human to cooperate is by understanding their skills and needs and addressing them in ways that build skills while meeting needs. Parents, teachers and others working with youth who know how to do this are referred to as brilliant. They understand how to get the best out of young people. But these practices must become mainstream. Why? Because in every situation adults are dealing with the whole person, not just the part they want to address. A teacher may have the most brilliant curriculum planned for her or his students but whether that teacher has the skills and brilliance to help students calm their emotions, and meet their social and creative needs, the brilliant curriculum is delivered but goes unlearned. Young people do not drop their intellectual self off to the classroom and then skip outside with their creative, emotional, social, and physical selves. It is not as though they have the capability to say, "load up all the information you want me to learn today and the rest of me will come pick my intellectual self up when you are done."

THE COGNITIVE SELF

The cognitive self is the self that thinks or uses mental processes to make language, memorize, analyze, synthesize, and hypothesize information. It also interprets information and makes decisions, ranging from easy to complex. Everyone has cognitive skills and the need to learn more cognitive skills. Cognitive needs change from moment to moment, from day to day, from month to month, from year to year.

THE CREATIVE SELF

The creative self is the self that makes something new out of already existing materials. Thinking outside the box to solve problems when facing challenges is also a sign of creativity. Creativity brings joy and fulfillment to human beings and is found in numerous forms, including art, dance, inventing treatments for illnesses, inventing items that make life more enjoyable, inventing sports activities, and designing and decorating everything from vehicles to homes to bedding, to educational materials. Everyone has creative skills, and the need to learn more about their unique creative qualities and be given the opportunities to develop the skills necessary to create in their own special way. Creative needs change from moment to moment, from day to day, from month to month, from year to year—because we grow, we develop, we learn, we discover, we explore!

THE EMOTIONAL SELF

The emotional self is the self that feels, (e.g., anger, joy, contentment, jealousy, apathy, etc.). Youth, like adults, experience different moods—different emotional states. Each of these emotional states is a part of the emotional self. Everyone has emotional skills and the need to learn more emotional skills. Emotional needs change from moment to moment, from day to day, from month to month, from year to year.

THE SOCIAL SELF

The social self is the self that interacts with others. This includes all types of communication—verbal and non-verbal—as well as social interactions which involve teamwork, competition or negotiation. Everyone has social skills and the need to learn more social skills. Social needs change from moment to moment, from day to day, from month to month, from year to year.

THE PHYSICAL SELF

The physical self is self that controls muscles, performs self-care tasks (e.g., toileting, resting, sleeping, grooming, eating, etc.) and is responsible for navigating our physical environment. Each individual has physical skills and the need to learn more physical skills. Physical needs change from moment to moment, from day to day, from month to month, from year to year.

There are many skills associated with each of the five-selves. For these skills to develop, caregivers must model those skills and provide learning opportunities for young people to practice and master them. It's also important to remember that the skills of these five selves are not all equally balanced in any individual. For example, we all know people who have amazing cognitive or intellectual skills, yet they lack social skills. Others have great social skills, but they aren't the brightest candle in the room. Some people are fantastic in sports, but they lack emotional intelligence and are unable to empathize with others. In these situations, skills are not balanced for all five-selves.

Most caregivers want young people to become well-rounded adults—equally skilled in all five-selves. But for this to happen each of the skills associated with the five-selves must be developed to their full *genetic* potential, and with the knowledge that every young person has their unique strengths and weaknesses. Most importantly, *every* young person must develop a self-image which acknowledges this imbalance and accepts it as being a *gift* instead of a handicap.

This is a formidable problem in Western Society, and probably beyond the scope of this book to cover. But it's worth mentioning that we reward and revere children with exceptional physical or intellectual gifts, but give very little formal recognition and status to children who have well-developed social and/or emotional skills. Children with brilliant creative minds or social skills often feel rejected or belittled by peers *and* adults, simply because they lack the athletic or intellectual capabilities of other children. This should never happen. Not because it's "mean" or "unfair," but because it's inconsistent with how great societies are built. Could you imagine a healthy society where everyone is a great intellectual, or where everyone is a great athlete, or where everyone is a great creative mind, or a great social influencer?

Athletes and entertainers who make millions of dollars a year would never make a dime if working people didn't pay to watch their movies, attend their sports events or go to their concerts. Great intellectual minds are often inspired by the work of poets, painters and/or fiction writers. They also need teachers, guidance counselors, pastors and spiritual leaders to help them overcome personal obstacles, heal from painful experiences and to learn the basic skills of reading, writing and arithmetic. It's important for young people to grasp this larger picture by valuing and accepting their personal gifts as their special way of *completing* the mosaic of our great society, instead of *competing* with other children who they see as "superior" to them.

If we're to encourage young people to develop each of their five selves and to become whole, we must do this within the context of preparing them to be a part of a "whole society." A whole society needs intellectually gifted people, creatively gifted people, emotionally gifted people, socially gifted people and physically gifted people, and this means each individual must learn to discover, accept and value their personal gifts, to use them to contribute to the wholeness of society *and* to accept and value people who are exceptionally gifted in other areas.

AN EXTRAORDINARY ILLUSTRATION OF THE FIVE SELVES IN ACTION

You can see an example of all five-selves at work simply by watching two young people play. They'll use language (cognitive), they'll pretend (creative), they'll express various emotions (emotional), and they'll move their bodies (physical). And of course, the interaction itself is a demonstration of the social self at work, completing the mosaic of the *whole self*. The way these skills overlap—and the way they are used as a young person develops into an adult—largely determines whether that young person will or won't live an extraOrdinary life.

Bullies are a prime example of a young person who hasn't developed the five selves in a balanced way. A verbal bully might abuse deceive or manipulate people with clever arguments because he/she lacks the social and emotional skills to engage in healthy negotiations. A physical bully pushes, overpowers or threatens other children because he/she lacks the social or intellectual skills to negotiate civilly. A social bully might use their ability to win friends and influence people to build cliques or triangles and to shut other children out. Social bullies often do this because they lack the skills to gain power and recognition through their intellectual achievements.

What happens when these bullies become parents, supervisors, politicians, neighbors, or community workers? Did you know that only 25 percent of bullies outgrow their bullying behaviors? They simply find more subtle or clever ways of imposing themselves on others. Have you ever seen an adult bully in a powerful position? I have, and it isn't pretty. Bullies destroy lives. Bullies create chaos. Bullies are dangerous. Bullies have low emotional intelligence. They lack empathy for others. They are deficit in emotional skill development. All because they haven't developed the five selves in a way which allows them to meet their needs without violating the boundaries of others.

Unfortunately, a lot of bullied children may grow up to become bullies themselves, out for revenge on the people who wronged them when they were young. This happens because these children aren't given the ability to develop into whole people during the years when they need it the most. Despite all of the years our children spend in school, we do not emphasize creative, emotional, and social skill development the way we should. We have removed all of the programs that support our creative young people—many of whom might have become our next great generation of movers and shakers. These young people are often marginalized and impeded from discovering what they were born to do in life.

These are the Abbeys of our society.

288

Abbey's biological father was a bully. But it doesn't take a bully to turn a child into an Abbey. Well-meaning parents and caregivers can do this simply because they lack the proper awareness, knowledge or training. When you think about how heavily our education system focuses on the intellectual and physical selves, it's easy to see why our society is full of invisible children. Imagine spending nine months of the year, five days a week, in a place (school), where you can't feel good about yourself, your accomplishments or who you truly are—simply because your natural gifts aren't a part of the standardized curriculum.

Imagine going home to family dysfunction, or to social injustice, or to a place where you aren't securely attached to anyone. And what would happen if you never received the consistent meaningful connections you needed? You'd never fully develop the intellectual, social, emotional and creative skills to understand your own needs well enough to communicate them to others, or even yourself. You'd never fully develop your unique skills and talents or learn how to turn them into a meaningful vocation.

Whether things got better for you or not, this childhood trauma would become encoded into your brain as you grew into a member of the adult community. You might go on to have a family of your own, where *your* children would now depend on you to give them what you yourself only have fragments of. This is how dysfunction gets passed from one generation to another. This is how young people with great dreams become the wandering generalities of our society, desperately clinging to jobs, hobbies, obsessions or relationships that only serve the purpose of filling their lives with noise so they don't have to hear the cry of their own unmet needs.

This is the reality for more than half the children in our society.

This is what life looks like when *you* are an Abbey.

What does this mean for the rest of us and for *our* children and their children and the future of their communities? What does it mean for adults who managed to mature into whole people, only to find themselves in a world where half the "adults" they interact with are children living in grown up bodies?

We should *all* have a *personal* interest in building meaningful connections with the young people in our care—no matter where we meet them or how brief our time with them is. All that is possible for a young person while they are alive can become a real and tangible expression of their truest potential. You can be a part of this. You can open the gate that leads all the dreams, hopes, and visions in a young person's heart out into the world where those dreams, hopes and visions can nurture and inspire others. And through each meaningful connection, you can send a ripple of compassion and contribution through our society that will carry on long after you're gone.

This requires a profound understanding of the five-selves and the skills associated with each one. Most importantly, it demands that we all change our perspective, raise our standards and see all our interactions with young people as an opportunity to give them our very best, by empowering them to discover and to become *their* very best.

Chapter 11:
Strategies for Developing the Five Selves

Cognitive Self

The cognitive self specializes in:

- Language

- Memory

- Perceiving and interpreting data, information, or stimuli

- Analyzing, hypothesizing, and synthesizing information to make decisions, or solve problems

These processes happen in the frontal lobe, which is why the frontal lobe must be engaged for appropriate reasoning to happen.

SKILLS

- Ability to remember information accurately.

- Ability to solve easy to complex problems.

- Ability to use verbal and written language appropriately.

- Ability to interpret language appropriately.

- Ability to communicate your needs, desires and feelings accurately.

- Ability to interpret stimuli in efficient, effective, socially appropriate ways.

- Critical thinking skills.

- Skills and accuracy in analyzing, hypothesizing, and synthesizing information.

TO DEVELOP THE COGNITIVE SELF

- Model appropriate cognitive skills.

- Provide learning opportunities to promote the development of any of the cognitive skills listed above.

- Provide age and ability appropriate opportunities for young people to engage in cognitive activities.

- Be the bridge to new cognitive skills—expand knowledge.

For example, to develop language skills, give your young person opportunities to practice reading, writing, speaking, and listening. To develop reasoning skills, provide opportunities for young people to reason through various situations. To develop memory skills, provide opportunities for your young person to work with mnemonic strategies. Whatever you want a young person to develop provide the opportunities and encouragement for them to develop it. Be patient. Not all kids learn the same and not all kids are going to "get it" immediately.

THE CREATIVE SELF

The creative self is the part of you that makes something novel and useful out of already existing materials.

SKILLS

Ability to create the following:

- Art
- Sculpture
- Cooking
- Movement
- Decorating
- Designing
- Inventing
- Problem solving (thinking outside of the box)

To Develop the Creative Self

- Model your own creativity (e.g., dancing, singing, cooking, sports, creative writing, scrapbooking; if it makes you happy, *do it!*).

- Provide opportunities for young people to create or to solve problems by thinking outside the box. Don't insist that they conform or follow your orders all the time. Instead, recognize what they are interested in and allow them to take the lead—this includes supporting and encouraging them as they pursue their interests.

- Use time-ins to explain, describe, and encourage creativity and creative problem solving.

Tip: Although youth enjoy crafts (making macaroni necklaces, etc.), too many times these activities stifle creativity by giving the young person a model to follow. Creativity is achieved when youth are given materials and allowed to do whatever they want without the fear of getting it "wrong." Giving them a model creates the need for them to confirm their work to fit the example given. This creates fear, and fear is an obstacle to creative thinking. Give them paper, paint brushes, and other materials, but don't give them an example of an item to copy. This way, they can create whatever they can imagine.

THE EMOTIONAL SELF

The emotional self is the part of you that feels emotions.

SKILLS

- Empathizing with others.

- Ability to read environ-mental cues appropriately.

- Emotional regulation: Controlling your emotionally driven behaviors.

- Ability to use the proper words to identify the need attached to an emotion.

- Ability to identify appropriate ways to get needs met.

- Ability to identify the place in your body where you feel an emotion.

TO DEVELOP THE EMOTIONAL SELF

- Model appropriate emotional skills. This includes regulating your emotional states and expressing them in an authentic, but safe manner.

- Provide learning opportunities to promote the emotional skills listed above. Provide age and ability appropriate opportunities and activities related to the emotional skills list. For example, to develop youth's emotional skills, give them opportunities to practice emotional regulation. For example, when youth are playing with others and they appear to have difficulty controlling their emotions, encourage them to count to five, wait, and use "I" statements instead of "you" statements to express their emotions. For example, "I am said," not "You made me sad" or "You're so depressing."

- Support youth in discovering where they feel, within their body, the emotion.

- Support youth in using a word to identify the emotion, or the unmet need, and to express an appropriate way to get the need met.

- Use time-ins to explain, describe, and encourage appropriate emotional skills (expressing empathy for others etc.).

Every emotion is attached to an unmet need. When we ask another person "I see you are angry, what do you need?" Many times, people get stuck describing their need in terms of what they want the other person to do "I just need him to be nice." But the other person's behavior is a completely separate thing from the need which makes us want them to behave that way.

For example, we don't really need everyone to be nice to us, we just don't want people being mean or cruel to us when we have done nothing to provoke them. Why? When people are mean and cruel to us it means they do not respect us or our differences. In other words, we have boundaries and expectations of others because of our basic need for respect.

The minute we suggest that someone, other than ourselves, behave in way to get our unmet need met, we give our personal power away. We maintain personal power when we refuse to see ourselves as a helpless victim and when we refuse to depend on another person to meet a need associated with a strong emotion. We can't make someone be nice to us. But, we can clearly state our boundaries with statements like, "I am not okay with you screaming at me. I find it disrespectful. If you need to scream, I will leave the room."

I have a dear friend. We have been friends now for over 30 years. But the friendship could have ended the year we met. This friend was always late. When she finally arrived, she made all her usual excuses. I forgave her because I wanted to have a good time—after all I had been waiting for over an hour. But I finally decided I'd had enough of her disrespecting my time. "To respect both of our schedules I need a call before I leave the house to meet you with an updated meeting time. If you are unable to do that, we will no longer be able to meet."

My constant acceptance of her tardy behavior delivered the message that I was okay with it. Once I spoke up, it became clear that I wasn't. My friend respected my request, but she also did a much better job at arriving on time so I wouldn't cancel our meeting. As it turned out she our time together as much as I did. We developed a wonderful very meaningful friendship that we both still treasure. This would have never happened if we hadn't established clear boundaries and expectations early on.

Likewise, we need to help young people develop the boundaries that leave them feeling good about themselves and their value as a person. We need to support them in being true to their values.

Nothing can achieve this better than meaningful connections. This is because meaningful connections help young people explore the needs behind their emotions so they can learn how to get those needs met. Young people who can do this understand their own boundaries. This allows them to be true to who they are and to like who they are. Most importantly, it empowers them to build a positive self-image.

THE SOCIAL SELF

The social self is the part of you that interacts with others through:

- Play
- Bonding
- Negotiation
- Conflict resolution

SKILLS

PROSOCIAL VS ANTISOCIAL BEHAVIORS:

- Sharing when it's appropriate but knowing appropriate ways to express when we do not want to share
- Self-assertion
- Compromising
- Perspective taking
- Waiting your turn
- Caring for others
- Sensitivity to diverse populations
- Ability to work effectively and efficiently with diverse. populations
- Ability to understand yourself and others.

To Develop the Social-Self

- Model appropriate social skills.

- Provide learning opportunities to promote the social skills listed above.

- Provide age and ability appropriate opportunities related to the social skills list. For example, to develop patience, give young people an opportunity to practice waiting their turn.

- Use time-ins to explain, describe, and encourage appropriate social interactions.

- Avoid permissive/indulgent parenting or caregiving.

The Physical Self

The physical self is the part of you that uses fine motor skills; uses gross motor skills; practices self-care (e.g., toileting oneself, resting, sleeping, grooming, eating, etc.); uses coordination; and navigates your physical environment.

SKILLS

- Eye-hand coordination activities.
- Large muscle activities
- Knowing when to rest, toilet, sleep
- Appropriate grooming
- Self-care
- Cardiovascular endurance
- Stamina
- Strength
- Flexibility
- Power
- Speed
- Coordination
- Agility
- Balance

"We have big dreams! We hope our caregivers can help us build the positive self-image we need to make our dreams come true. We want to live the lives we intentionally choose, rather than a life we unintentionally fall into. We want to live ExtraOrdinary lives!"

To Develop the Social Self

- Model healthy physical skills and correct body mechanics.

- To promote the development of any of the skills listed, provide age and ability appropriate opportunities related to the list above.

- For example, to develop youth's flexibility, give them opportunities to practice stretching.

Chapter 12: The Brain—Where Learning Happens

We could change the world in the most remarkable way if we just used strategies which promote healthy brain development in young people. Surely, you know how much emphasis we put on physical development. If your new born baby came home from the hospital only being able to move his body from the waist up, you'd be rushing back to the hospital without a second thought. Yet, because brain development isn't readily visible, and harder to measure, we are less aware of whether our child is reaching their full brain development potential. We assume that as long as they learn to talk, to read and eventually to write and to do arithmetic, things are okay.

But what about their unique, creative potential? What about their development of a strong and healthy self-image, and the other qualities and skills we've talked about in this book? All the great people you read about in history books had highly developed thinking skills; skills which went beyond the ordinary talking, reading, writing and basic math. That's what

304

made these people great. Imagine all the incredible potential we're throwing away because our young people are not developing vital creative, emotional and social skills or the qualities inherent of a positive self-image.

More importantly, think about the kind of society we'd miss out on by not making the development of these skills and qualities a priority. Things may seem good enough, but a society is only as strong as its weakest link. Unless these skills become a priority, a LOT of *potential* geniuses will go through their entire lives never realizing who they were born to be. We don't know where the next great Edison, or the next Steve Jobs or the next Mother Theresa will come from. But by making these things a priority, we can ensure that every young person gets the opportunity to discover their own potential and to make the most of who they are. This starts with learning how to help young people develop their brain to its fullest potential.

THE IMPACT OF CAREGIVING ON YOUTH BRAIN DEVELOPMENT

The study, or science, of human development (HD) provides us with valuable information about ourselves and others. More importantly, it shows us how one person's behavior impacts other people's behavior, for better or for worse. And of course, the impact of a teacher, firefighter, nurse, doctor, or inventor on the lives of others is extremely different from the impact of a rapist, murderer, pedophile, gang member, or drug dealer.

I'm around young people every day. Never once have I heard any of them say, "When I grow up I'm going to be a heroin addict, a murderer, a thief, a pedophile, a gang member, a drug dealer, homeless, mentally ill, an alcoholic, or a menace to society." Almost all young people start out with wonderful dreams for their future. What happens to make them stop believing in these dreams and to become a person they never wanted to become?

Do we believe that all criminals are the result of genetics? In some rare cases this is true, but typically human thinking and behavior is shaped by a combination of genetics and environment. While a person may have the genetic predisposition to be sociopathic, some environmental situations can trigger the sociopathic behaviors. While some may be predisposed to addictive types of behaviors, there is no doubt that society, and its cultural norms, has a significant impact as to whether these addictive tendencies take control of the person.

The statement "Youth are like sponges," is about as true a statement as you'll find about human development. Think of a young person's brain like cookie dough. When it's raw, even the slightest pressure or impression can change its shape. But once cooked, that shape becomes practically impossible to change without breaking the cookie. Likewise, young people start learning who they are long before they start their formal education. They're learning whether they're important, valued, respected, capable, loved unconditionally, and worthy. They're forming their self-image based on the information their caregivers deliver to them. Their self-image impacts their motivation, drive, belief in what they can and can't do and therefore is pivotal in developing the cognitive, creative, emotional, social, and physical skills they will use throughout their entire lives. It's much easier to shape these positive character traits early on than to try and break negative ones later.

This is why early learning has a tremendous impact on future learning, thinking, decisions, judgments, and behavior. In fact, early learning sets up the architecture of the brain, including hard wiring for the mental models we use to evaluate the world, ourselves and others. These models, whether they're positive or negative, will influence our perceptions and attitudes about every situation we face. To summarize, you might say that early learning plants the seeds for future living.

EARLY LEARNING—WHY THE EARLY YEARS ARE SO POWERFUL

A newborn's brain is already a quarter the size it will be when the baby is a full grown adult. By the age of five, that same brain will weigh 95 percent of what it will when the baby is an adult. This is nearly a 400 percent increase in brain size of the first five years of a child's life. Just imagine that amount of learning that happens over those first five years. This is ALL before the first year of formal education begins. And what is the baby learning? They're learning from the experiences and environment provided to them by their caregivers. They learn from negative experiences and they learn from positive ones. And think about who is providing these learning experiences, whether it be the adults at home, at school, or in their community. These adults contribute immensely to the most accelerated learning period of the little person's life.

But that's not all. The learning that happens during these first five years is also "formatting" the brain for future learning. This is more important than the raw information the young person is taking in. The wiring determines *how* the brain learns to think, to assess and to react to the environment. It shapes the thinking patterns which determine the brain's habits. So, whatever we want our youth to learn, it is important that we also know how to hardwire their brains during this first five years. For example, if you want your youth to be kind:

1. Model and encourage kindness.

2. Provide learning opportunities for them to demonstrate kindness. When you catch them being kind, say: "You were kind when you helped your sister."

3. If you catch them being unkind, ask them, "Was that kind? What choice could you make that *is* kind?"

If you want your youth to be ethical:

1. Model and encourage ethical behaviors.

2. Provide learning opportunities for them to demonstrate ethical behavior. When you catch them being ethical, say: "You showed honesty by not keeping the extra money the clerk gave you. You decided to stay true to your values and your beliefs."

3. If you catch them doing something unethical, ask them, "Was that ethical? What choice could you make that *is* ethical?"

If you want your youth to develop positive thinking habits:

1. Model and encourage positive self-image behaviors.

2. Provide learning opportunities for them to build a positive self-image.

3. Use the strategies in the *Positive Youth Guidance System* to encourage behaviors that will promote positive self-image.

To sum up, remember that young people are like sponges. They soak up information based on their interactions with their primary caregivers. This starts the moment they're born and it continues throughout their childhood. This is why parents, teachers, families, and other caregivers should master these simple practices and strategies.

The Anatomy of the Brain

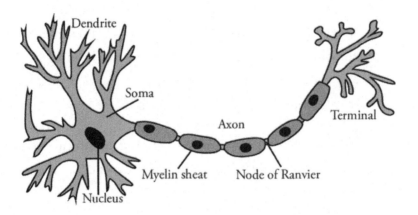

The Neuron (Where Learning Happens and Habits Are Formed)

The neuron is the basic working unit of the brain—a specialized cell designed to transmit information to other nerve cells, muscles, or gland cells.

The communication between neurons allows humans to learn, think, see, hear, experience tactile sensations, smell, taste, control bodily functions, and engage in voluntary (chosen behaviors) and involuntary behaviors (breathing, heartbeats, etc.).

Why Is the Brain Capable of Learning?

- The brain is built for learning because it is the only way to ensure our survival.

- The neuroplasticity of the brain allows for the tremendous amount of learning that is necessary for humans to adjust their thinking and behavior according to the environments they inhabit. Youth learn early that a lion in the zoo is not to be feared, but if they saw one running toward them on the street, they would scream and run.

NEUROPLASTICITY

1. Neuroplasticity is the process by which our brain's neural synapses and pathways are altered due to environmental, behavioral, and neural changes.

2. Neuroplasticity allows the brain to reorganize itself by forming new neural connections from already existing ones and to continually develop neural pathways. We call this process *learning*.

3. Previously it was believed that the human brain is hardwired at the time we are born. This would mean that at the time of our birth we would have a set of unchangeable cognitive abilities and tendencies which would remain with us throughout life. If this were true, humans would not be able to adapt to their living environment and to survive and reproduce.

4. Neuroplasticity ensures the brain's survival by helping it adapt to its environment.

HOW THE BRAIN LEARNS

- We are born with billions of neurons. Each neuron has several structures that are underdeveloped at birth. These structures begin to develop when certain environmental experiences are provided—caregivers provide many of these experiences.

- Two very important structures of neurons are axons and dendrites. These structures are essential for neurons to communicate with each other. Axons send messages, and dendrites receive messages.

- The important thing that caregivers must understand is that by age three, the axons and dendrites that have not developed (because they have not had the experiences they need in order to develop) *prune* themselves, and become useless.

- In real life, this means youth who have never experienced kindness will not develop the axons and dendrites related to kindness. They will not have a mental model of kindness.

- When humans are exposed to the same information repeatedly (whether they intentionally or unintentionally want the exposure), they *learn*. In other words we may intentionally choose to remember information, or we may repeatedly hear something about ourselves from caregivers and unintentionally assimilate that information. Once information is learned at the neural level, it is difficult to unlearn. In fact, we don't unlearn information—even when we forget it out of a lack of use. This truth shows itself when humans develop habits. Habits are the result of repeated exposure to information which eventually creates a neural pathway in the brain. These habits are triggered by something that occurs in the environment (stimuli). If you eat to soothe yourself when you are nervous, nervousness becomes your stimuli (trigger) for eating, and you eventually form the habit of nervous eating.

- Young people form habits too. Whether these habits are healthy and appropriate or unhealthy and inappropriate has everything to do with their caregivers—particularly between birth and the age of five years. Though the window is always open for learning, it becomes difficult to unlearn information which has "downloaded" itself into the brain.

THE BRAIN IS ANALOGOUS TO A COMPUTER HARD DRIVE

- Once a programmer downloads information onto the hard drive of a computer, it's hard to get rid of it without professional help from a computer technician.

- Computers can accidentally or unintentionally be victims of people who intentionally or unintentionally download viruses.

- Viruses mess up the way a computer responds to its users.

In other words, information programmed into our brain, doesn't get unprogrammed and it doesn't matter whether we *want* this programming to happen or not. Any information we're exposed to by repetition or within the context of a highly emotional experience can become a permanent part of our wiring. Of course, adults with well-developed brains have "virus protection," (i.e., critical thinking, positive beliefs etc.) to guard themselves against bad or unwanted information. But a young person's brain is just as exposed as a lap top when it's logged in to an insecure internet connection with no firewall or virus protection. This is how a developing brain gets programed by his/her caregivers—and the information it's programmed with can be good or bad. Therefore, we must *proactively* expose young people's brains to information that will benefit them *and* equip them to guard themselves against bad information and destructive ideas.

CHAPTER 13: AGE-SPECIFIC COMMUNICATION STRATEGIES

COMMUNICATION TIPS FOR ALL AGES

1. **Model Appropriate Communication.** Remember that youth learn best when we model the behaviors we

want them to learn. By doing this, we also give them opportunities to learn different skill sets. For example, if we want youth to learn appropriate communication, we must model appropriate communication. This means yelling, screaming, putdowns, humiliating, and other inappropriate tactics should be avoided.

2. **Provide Learning Opportunities.** Mistakes are terrific learning experiences. If you put your foot in your mouth, or if your young person does, don't go into meltdown mode. Treat it as a learning experience.

3. **Choose Time-ins, Rather Than Time-outs.** A time-in is better than a time-out. It allows you to discuss, lead, cue, and guide your young person to the discovery of appropriate communication methods.

4. **Use Positive Tone and Body Language.** Positive tone and body language are important when you're guiding your young person through a learning experience. These non-verbals tell your young person that you understand them, that you trust them and that you believe they're capable of learning and doing better. Negative tone and/or body language deliver the opposite message, even if you had something different in mind when you chose your words.

5. **Create Safe Opportunities for Youth to Express Their Feelings.** If your child is angry, try a positive response like this, "Go in the bathroom and scream as

loud as you can for one minute," instead of a punitive response like, "Stop yelling."

COMMUNICATION STRATEGIES: BIRTH TO TWO YEARS

1. Touch.

2. Cuddle.

3. Croon.

4. Tell babies what you are doing. "I'm changing your diaper now. Now I'm sprinkling powder on to keep you nice and dry."

5. Tone and body language matter (babies read emotions).

6. Stay physically connected.

7. Choose baby first. Put down the cell phone.

8. Have two-way conversations (sing, rhyme) and invite babies to respond.

9. Use sounds and words to help them develop language skills. If your toddler says, "Bye, bye," you might extend his thought by saying, "You want to go bye, bye with Mommy? We will leave soon."

10. Babies understand touch, whether you're paying attention to them, or responding to their physical needs. Your kind responses tell a baby that they matter. These gestures also help your baby learn to attach feelings and thoughts to sounds.

COMMUNICATION STRATEGIES: TWO YEARS TO FIVE YEARS

1. Preschoolers can understand your feelings, but they're not ready to link them to complex verbal descriptions. So, use simple language to explain your feelings to them. "I feel sad when you bite a playmate." This way, you're demonstrating self-awareness by labeling and expressing your feelings.

2. When you express your feelings in the appropriate format, you teach your child an appropriate way of expressing their feelings. You can encourage young children to express their own emotions with simple questions like, "Tell me how you felt when you bit your classmate."

3. Ask for your preschooler's help in figuring out a problem. For example, if you find out they've bit a playmate, you might say, "Did you want to be first in line, but it was Tommy's turn?" If they don't answer, try following up with, "Could it have been that you were angry because it wasn't your turn?"

4. Youngsters need help learning to label their emotions. You can help them by asking them to put their feelings into words. To do this, just read their emotions and use questions like, "You wanted to be line leader, didn't

you? You were mad. Can you use your words to tell me, 'I was mad'?"

5. Help your preschooler develop self-awareness (emotional awareness of the situation). Even if there is misbehavior, show them that you can talk about it together. Most preschoolers can understand a sentence like "Sometimes, I get mad too. But our teeth are for chewing our food, not biting our playmates" or like, "When I get mad, I focus on counting to ten. That helps me."

6. Offer them limited choices. Too many choices can be overwhelming and make it difficult for them to choose anything.

7. Don't end your sentence with, "Okay?" as it just invites the child to argue with you. Asking your child if an activity is okay can lead to a lengthy discussion or a power struggle.

8. Don't overexplain. Simple explanations may be more effective than long discussions. If your preschooler is having a tantrum, you can hold her close, or simply stay near her. Sometimes this "says" more than you can say with words.

COMMUNICATION STRATEGIES: SIX YEARS TO ELEVEN YEARS

1. Find time to talk. With a school-age child, you'll have fewer opportunities for conversation as you did when they were a preschooler. As your child grows, she may turn to you less frequently, so you may need to make a special effort to spend time with her.

2. Speak to your school-age child in a mature fashion. School-age young people want their "bigness" acknowledged. They may be offended if they feel they're being spoken to like a baby (even if they happen to be acting like one). You might say, "I expect you to begin your book report. What time would you like to work on it?" Rather than saying, "How many times do I have to tell you to do your book report?"

3. Show your school-age child respect. For example, your child asks for something, before saying no, you might ask them to help you understand their needs. They may have information you don't. Your inquiry acknowledges that you respect your child's needs even though you may need to say no.

4. Ask your school-age child specific, rather than general questions. Instead of asking a question such as, "How was school?" you might ask, "Did your teacher write any comments on your science project?" Also, avoid

leading questions. A query such as, "Do you think it's appropriate to talk to me that way?" often backfires. Instead, you might say, "Is there a different way you can talk to me so I can hear you better?"

5. Listen to your school-age child without contradicting them. Instead of saying, "That's ridiculous," you might simply say, "Hmm," or "Really?" Then ask specific questions based on the situation your child has described.

6. Repeat what your child says, but use more mature wording. For example, you can rephrase their statement as a question which implies that you're asking them whether you understand them. In this way, you are respecting your child's intelligence, making them feel understood and encouraging them to tell you more. For example, you might say, "So, you think your gym teacher is stupid, but you don't want me to 90-8

7. intervene? Can you tell me what you are upset about?"

8. Laugh a little and admit your mistakes. At times, humor is the best way to resolve a dispute, react to an upset, or make a request of your school-age child. You can also ask your child for help in figuring out what to do. Young people love to hear parents admit they're wrong. You might say, "Am I making a mess of this? Should we try to figure it out a different way?"

9. Ask your child to help set his own limits. Don't be afraid to say no when they need to hear it—or when you need to say it. You might even let your child make the rules sometimes. For instance, you might ask him to propose a reasonable time to begin his homework. "Discuss it and then back off," recommends Gillian McNamee, PhD. "Ask your child to be the boss in deciding what help is given, how much and when (in accordance with her teacher's instructions)." In this way, you help your child feel in control of their own world.

10. Keep talking, even if your school-age child won't talk to you. Don't give up or retaliate by stonewalling them. "You will feel at times that you have lost your credibility with a school-age child," comments Michael Thompson, PhD. "If you take silence or impulsive remarks personally, things can go quite badly. Youth are often simply trying to establish their independence."

MELTDOWNS

I have two questions:

1. Do you ever get mad?

2. Do you ever get really, really mad?

Think about when someone cuts you off on the road and almost takes your fender off, and you think to yourself, *"I should have just stepped on the gas pedal and smashed into the jerk!"*

If you get this mad as an adult, you bet your young person does too! However, they don't always have the emotional control to stop a tantrum or a screaming fit because they have not developed self-regulation. They just want to be heard! So here are some things to keep in mind when your child acts out:

- They need you to stop and listen to their words.

- They need to learn to be aware of their volatile emotional states.

- Self-awareness allows you to remain in touch with your emotions before they escalate. Young people don't always have this luxury.

TALKING THROUGH ANGRY FEELINGS

Let your young person express negative feelings, and don't judge them for having them. Imagine if you expressed an important concern to a work supervisor, a friend, or your partner and they replied, "You shouldn't say that," or, "You really don't mean that," or, "Do it because I'm the boss and I gave you an order." These comments are dismissive and leave the other person feeling unimportant and disrespected. Such comments can also make the person even more negative, and the situation can escalate.

Of course, sometimes angry young people seem completely out of reach. But the right response can deescalate the situation and invite them into a reasonable dialog about their anger. The secret is to understand that most angry people have a deep need to be heard and understood without judgment. That said, here are a few ways to deescalate angry outbursts:

- When a preschooler or younger child screams, yells, bites, kicks, or has a tantrum, when in public remove the child from the situation, (e.g., go outside of the restaurant or create distance between others and you and your child) without yelling, scolding, or lecturing them. Once there is distance established, use a calm voice, "When you are calm, I'm ready to hear your words. I can see you are upset. Use your words and tell me what made you feel that way."

- When a school-aged child throws a tantrum, "I can see how frustrated you are. You are free to meet your need on your own, or I can help you."

- Youth can make comments that hurt our feelings, and we can respond with statements such as: "Oh my, that hurt my feelings," but when we respond wit, "I can see you are upset. Let's talk" you are providing an opportunity for a young person to identify their emotion and connect it to a need." This is a critical communication skill to be learned, practiced, and honed.

You can prevent future outbursts or inappropriate behaviors by setting proactive rules like this in your home or classroom:

For Younger Children

- Hands are for soft touches.
- Our teeth are for chewing our food.
- In the house, we use walking feet.
- Use inside voices when in the house.
- Our toys are to play with.

For youth of all ages:

- We talk kindly about others or we don't speak about them.
- We are kind.
- We are honest.
- We are respectful.
- We are courageous.

- We are creative.
- We are wise problem solvers.
- We persist despite challenges.
- We each have our own special light.

Note: Remember you are free to choose your rules and modify them as needed. A smart way to use posted rules is to remind young people when they are breaking one and it gives you the opportunity to give them the opportunity to choose a more appropriate behavior. For example, your son is angry with his sister and saying unkind remarks to her, you might say, "Do we have a rule about kindness? Are you being kind? How can you deliver your message in a kind way?" This sentence provides learning opportunities to both kids, whereas a statement to your son like "You apologize to your sister right now," does not.

You can also help youth learn to communicate when they're angry by modeling appropriate communication skills. For example, instead of storming around the house with a scowl on your face, slamming doors/cabinets or giving your family the silent treatment, try making self-awareness statements about your anger, like "I'm really frustrated about the situation at work, which means I really must think about what I need so I can address it appropriately. Talk the way you think yourself through emotional situations. It is also okay to include in your young person in the brain storming process of identifying the need, and ideas as to how to get the need met appropriately. You can even report back the results.

This technique connects you with youth in many ways, but mostly it allows them to see that adults have challenges just like young people and the same strategy can be used by both.

Most importantly, you can listen to your young person and give them a chance to honestly express the reason for their anger or frustration. You can do that with questions like:

- Why do you think it isn't fair?
- What do you need me to understand?
- What do you think should happen?

When listening to your young person's responses, it's important that you're not thinking about what you want to say next. Remember, angry people want to be heard and understood without judgment. If you're planning your response while your young person is still talking, you're not really listening to them—you're listening to your own internal dialogue.

If a young person suspects that you're not really interested in their response, they'll stop answering you and go right back to acting out. But if they feel heard and understood, they'll have a chance to hear their own descriptions of their emotional states and the needs behind those emotions. In time, this will help them find a way to get outside their anger and focus on solving problems and learning from their challenges.

To Adults: Things I Do before I Flip My Lid with a Kid...

When a young person says or does something annoying and I feel the emotion bubbling up inside of me:

- I remind myself that anger, frustration, and other similar emotions drop my IQ by about 50%...so I shut myself up until I reconnect my limbic system with my frontal lobe.

- I excuse myself from the situation. I might say, "I'm uncomfortable with the direction this conversation is heading right now. I need to stop talking and discuss this another time. Let's try this again later.

- I remind myself that winning is overrated. My sanity is much more valuable than being right. It is okay to listen to our youth and simply reply, "I need to think about what you said, and once I have, we will talk again." Set a reasonable timeline so you can process the situation and respond when your IQ is at peak performance.

Note: When your nine-year-old or teen says, "Mom, I can't discuss this now. I need to get my head around the situation," you will know you are doing a great job.

Chapter 14: Discipline Styles—The Good, the Bad, and the Ugly

Caring for young people can be a paradox. On one hand, you want them to follow rules, to do their homework and chores, and to behave in safe and socially acceptable ways. On the other hand, you don't want to squelch their inquisitive nature. After all, it's this nature that drives them to learn through curiosity, exploration, and discovery. You also don't want to crush their motivation with embarrassing or humiliating punishments.

How in the world are you supposed to do *both* at the same time?

The answer lies in how you discipline your youth. There are a few different forms of discipline. The ideal form is what I call *Positive Youth Guidance*. We identify this style in the *Positive Youth Guidance System*. In Part I of this chapter, I'll describe the differences between positive youth guidance and punishment. In Part II of this chapter, we'll talk about the difference between natural consequences and logical consequences. These two forms of discipline can work together to shape young people's behaviors and protect their natural curiosity, all while developing a positive self-image, self-regulation, and self-efficacy.

PART 1: POSITIVE DISCIPLINE VS. PUNISHMENT

POSITIVE DISCIPLINE

VS.

PUNISHMENT

"There is a difference between positive discipline and punishment."

WHAT IS PUNISHMENT?

For most parents, punishment is just a means of trying to get their child to stop doing something and/or to start doing something else. It might include smacking, arm pulling, glaring, scolding, shouting, threatening, put downs, cruel teasing, limiting or restricting participation, or withdrawing affection. For the sake of this discussion, we'll call these actions "imposed consequences." The problem is, even when imposed consequences work, they're often humiliating and embarrassing for the child. A punished child feels like less of a person. This is why punishment is a double-edged sword. It makes the child feel bad, and it's this "feeling bad" that makes the child stop the behavior. That's why parents keep using imposed consequences and, of course, they expect this approach to keep working.

The problem is that these expectations conflict with the long-term outcomes the punishment produces. This is because the imposed consequences prevent the child from learning to respond to *natural consequences*. Instead of learning that *their* actions have natural consequences, they learn that "mommy will make me feel bad if I do _____."

CONSEQUENCES OF PUNISHMENT

Trust me, Mom, I hear you ... but all this humiliation is bad for my self-image!

- It doesn't work when the adult is not present and the child believes they can get away with the behavior.

This happens because, as the adult is removed, so is the child's fear of the imposed consequences.

- Punishment impedes healthy relationship building between the young person and their punitive caregiver.

- Because young people aren't experiencing the natural consequences of their actions, they're not developing self-awareness that provokes self-regulation and self-control.

- The humiliating nature of the punishment often damages the young person's self-esteem.

- Punishment models inappropriate aggression, giving the child the idea that someone who is bigger, stronger, older and more verbally adept has the right to abuse them.

- Children are sometimes punished because of unreasonable or unclear expectations.

So, to summarize, punishment is the deliberate application of imposed consequences in an attempt to modify a young person's behavior. Even when it "works," punishment fails to help the child mature into a self-governing adult.

Part 2: Natural Consequences and Logical Consequences

What Are Natural Consequences?

A natural consequence is something that happens as the natural result of a specific behavior. For example, if a child forgets to bring his lunch to school, the child will be hungry. The hunger is the natural consequence of the child forgetting to bring his lunch to school. Another example is a teen who does not study for her exam and who earns a low score. The low score on the exam is the natural consequence of not studying.

Many caregivers use these natural consequences as a discipline strategy. They rely on the natural order of the world as a means of teaching their young people the consequences of their actions. These caregivers don't need to do anything other than allow the natural consequence of a child's behavior to occur, and to help the child understand how their choices led to the consequences and how they can use this knowledge to create better outcomes in the future. Of course, some natural consequences are too severe to use as learning experiences. If your child is about to run in front of a car, you don't let them get hit just so they can learn a lesson. It's also possible to misuse these natural consequences as punishments rather than as learning experiences. But we'll talk about how to deal with that paradox in a few moments.

NATURAL CONSEQUENCES AS POSITIVE DISCIPLINE OR AS PUNISHMENT

For a natural consequence to be effective, you must communicate effectively with your young person (e.g., "you were hungry because of the natural consequence of forgetting your lunch).

The *way* you *deliver* information about the natural consequence determines whether it is positive discipline or punishment.

- Adults who choose to *deliver* the information about the natural consequence in a positive discipline format, encourage, asks questions, and demonstrates trust their trust in the child. For example, "you were hungry because as a natural consequence of leaving your lunch at home. What can you do tomorrow to help you remember?").

- Adults who choose to *deliver* the information about the natural consequence in a punitive format shame, embarrass, humiliate, degrade, or cruelly tease the child. For example, "you deserved to be hungry for leaving your lunch at home. I bet you won't do that again").

DELIVERY OF NATURAL CONSEQUENCE: POSITIVE DISCIPLINE VS PUNISHMENT

Situations:

Teen is upset about a low grade. *Using a Natural Consequence as Positive Discipline:* Calm voice: "I know you are unhappy with your grade. How can you do better the next time?" *Using a Natural Consequence as a Punishment:* Angry voice: "You deserve that F. Stop crying. You did it to yourself."

Child isn't getting dressed for school. *Using a Natural Consequence as Positive Discipline:* Calm voice: "Do you want to go to school in your pajamas or your play clothes? It is your choice. We are leaving the house immediately after our breakfast routine." *Using a Natural Consequence as a Punishment:* Angry voice: "I'll drag you to school in your pajamas if you don't get dressed immediately!"

As you can see from the above, natural consequences allow a young person to learn from the natural order of the world. Some caregivers might assume that allowing their child to go hungry because they forgot their lunch is cruel. But this work does not intend for a caregiver to starve a child. One missed meal doesn't constitute starvation. Children whose health is at risk for missing a meal and preschoolers are not expected to go hungry for forgetting their lunch. Preschool is a time period in which youngsters prepare for formal education routines and expectations. To be clear a natural consequence should never be allowed when a child's health or safety is at risk.

NATURAL CONSEQUENCES CANNOT BE USED IN ALL SITUATIONS

Caregivers cannot use natural consequences *if the health or safety of the child is involved. We aren't going to allow a child to run into the street and be hurt.* In this situation you would take the child aside and use a time-in. A time-in is the reverse of a time-out. It's when you take time to explain the logical reason for your decisions and your boundaries. For example, if a child begins to run in the street you can jump up and grab the child to protect them from being hurt. Once they're safe, you use a time-in by saying something like "You can stay by my side, since you ran into the street. When you decide you will not go into the street, you are free to leave my side."

WHAT ARE LOGICAL CONSEQUENCES

A logical consequence logically follows a child's behavior. For example, if you want your child to complete his homework immediately after school, there is a logical consequence if they do not. Like natural consequences, logical consequences can be delivered as either positive discipline or as a punishment. For example, consider this punishment related statement: "You won't go out to play until your homework is completed." But using *positive discipline* you might say, "Feel free to go outside and play as soon as your homework is completed." Notice that both statements mean the same thing, but the latter statement is framed in a positive direction which is much more likely to create a calm interaction for both you and your child.

GUIDELINES ON USING LOGICAL CONSEQUENCES

Based on research published by Virginia Cooperative Extension, Virginia Tech, and Virginia State University (May 1, 2009)

- Logical consequences are arranged by parents.

- The consequence must logically follow the child's behavior (e.g., "If you do ___, then ___ will happen").

- Logical consequences work when the child is trying to get the parent's attention by misbehaving (procrastinating, ignoring rules).

- Consequences are learning experiences, not punishments.

- Using logical consequences takes practice and patience. It is hard to identify logical consequences, and it is hard to *not* intervene when you can save the day and help your child avoid discomfort.

- We use logical consequences to help a child learn to make decisions and to be responsible for their own behaviors.

- Avoid using logical consequences when you're angry. Use a calm voice and don't end the sentence with, "Okay?"

Remember, once you use the word *okay,* you have invited the child to say, "No, it isn't okay!"

- Using logical consequences delivers powerful messages to young people. You're saying, "I trust you and have confidence that you can think for yourself."

- When stated properly, logical consequences give the child a choice. For example…

  - Example of no choice: "Do your homework or you can't go out and play." This statement is inappropriate because you're telling the young person what to do instead of introducing them to a logical consequence.

  - Example of choice: "Sarah, feel free to go outside and play as soon as your homework is complete." This statement is right because it makes the *consequence* the culprit, *not the caregiver.* By connecting the consequence to "Sarah's" actions, you're giving her a choice.

COMPARING POSITIVE DISCIPLINE AND PUNISHMENT

1. *Positive Discipline:* It works. *Punishment:* It works.

2. *Positive Discipline:* Takes time, patience, specific knowledge. *Punishment:* Fast, uses blame, shame, intimidation.

ExtraOrdinary Youth

3. *Positive Discipline:* Builds and supports self-awareness, self-regulation, and self-control. *Punishment:* Thwarts self-awareness, self-regulation, and self-control.

4. *Positive Discipline:* Builds and supports positive self-image. *Punishment:* Harms positive self-image.

5. *Positive Discipline:* Builds and supports self-esteem. *Punishment:* Harms self-esteem.

6. *Positive Discipline:* Builds and supports strong sense of self-efficacy. *Punishment:* Harms strong sense of self-efficacy.

7. *Positive Discipline:* Promotes quality interactions between youth and caregiver. *Punishment:* Discourages quality interactions between youth and caregiver.

8. *Positive Discipline:* Promotes self-motivating behaviors (youth are not afraid of being humiliated if they mess up). *Punishment:* Discourages self-motivating behaviors (Youth are fearful of messing up and of being humiliated or scolded by caregiver).

9. *Positive Discipline:* Youth learn to think for themselves when caregivers are not around. This way, they tend to do the right thing without being told. Positive discipline explains issues to children, and this builds their cognitive skills. *Punishment:* Youth may misbehave when caregivers are not around because they haven't learned to think through situations. They only

fear getting caught. Parents don't explain issues, and young people are not given the opportunities to learn thinking skills and to guide their own behaviors.

The Differences between Logical Consequences and Punishment

1. *Logical Consequences:* Calm tone of voice and matter-of-fact body language. *Punishment:* Angry tone of voice and/or body language.

2. *Logical Consequences:* Friendly but firm attitude. *Punishment:* Hostile or aggressive attitude.

3. *Logical Consequences:* Willing to accept youth's choices. *Punishment:* Unwilling to offer youth choices.

Virginia Cooperative Extension, Virginia Tech, and Virginia State University (May 1, 2009)

Logical Consequences with Positive Guidance vs Punishment

1. Youth ignores house rule: No outside play until homework is completed. *Logical Consequence with Positive Child Guidance:* Calmly: "Rihanna, feel free to go outside and play with your friends as soon as you finish your homework." *Logical Consequence with Punishment:* Angry: "There is no way you are going outside to play. You know the rule—no homework, no

playing! If you don't get to go outside, it's your own fault!"

2. Your child hurts another child while playing outside. *Logical Consequence with Positive Child Guidance:* First, check to be certain the other child is okay. Next calmly use a time-in to address the aggressor. "Derek, I need you to come in the house." Allow Derek time to calm down before talking to him. Young people cannot problem-solve when they're angry. Then, use the time-in by saying: "Use your own words and tell me what happened. I see you are angry. It's okay to be angry, but it isn't okay to hurt others. What could you do the next time you get angry?" Discuss coping strategies for anger, then say: "Tell me when you are ready to go outside and try again." *Logical Consequence with Punishment:* Angry: "Derek, get in this house right now! I saw you, and there is no excuse for that behavior. No more outside play for you today!"

Chapter 15:
Insecure vs Secure Attachment

By Penny G. Davis MA

Attachment

What is attachment, and why is it important? Attachment between caregivers and infants has been studied since the 1930s. It started with John Bowlby, who first looked at infants and mothers who, because of hospitalization, were separated during the first three months of the infant's life. Mary Ainsworth and Mary Main added to Bowlby's work, as did dozens of other researchers who have worked diligently on the topic since the 1990s.

Thanks to this research, we now know that secure attachment is foundational to our mental health and well-being. We know that young people who don't get responsive, consistent, and congruent care during their early years are at higher risk for various physical, social and emotional problems. We also know that secure attachment is essential to a young person's brain development and their ability to self-regulate.

343

Most importantly, the research has revealed that young people who don't develop secure attachments are more likely to gravitate towards relationships which further destabilize their emotional and social development.

For example, the Adverse Childhood Experiences (ACE) research done by Dr. Vincent Felitti at Kaiser Permanente in San Diego, California, examined more than seventeen thousand participants eighteen years of age or older. The researchers defined "adverse childhood experiences" as one or more of the following:

- **Three Types of Abuse:** 1) sexual, 2) verbal, or 3) physical.

- **Four Types of Family Dysfunction:** 1) a mentally ill or alcoholic parent, 2) a mother who is a domestic violence victim, 3) an incarcerated family member, or 4) a parent who is absent as a result of divorce or abandonment.

- **Two Types of Neglect:** 1) emotional or 2) physical.

Participants were scored one point for each one of the above experiences, with zero being the lowest possible score and nine being the highest. The results revealed that participants with scores of four or more were at much higher risk for developing a host of physical illnesses. They also showed increased risk of drug and/or alcohol addiction, depression, suicide, etc. More importantly, they were found to be much more likely to attach to caregivers who had suffered similar experiences (Felitti et al, 1998).

I like to think of attachment as an invisible string connecting us to others. Think of the people in your life with whom you feel close. Would you say you are attached to them? If so, what tells you that you are attached? Does the attachment disappear when the other person is in a different city or country? Does it disappear if they die? I think most of us will agree that it doesn't. We remain connected to our loved ones, even if they no longer inhabit this earth. We think about them, perhaps visit their grave, or a place that was once special to them. Some of us even talk to them when we need help or support.

Attachment is a general term which describes the state and quality of one person's ties to another (Becker-Weidman & Shell 2011). According to Main and Solomon (n.d.), secure attachment isn't just about love; it's also about survival and self-regulation. How does attachment happen? Contrary to early "bonding" studies, it doesn't happen at birth or in the few hours after. Attachment is a process which takes place during the early days, weeks, and months of an infant's life. This process causes the infant's brain to develop in such a way that they can eventually acquire the skill of self-regulation *and* develop the ability to seek out and to build and sustain healthy attachments throughout their childhood and adult life.

THE PROCESS OF ATTACHMENT

From the moment of birth, babies are making decisions about who they are, how the world works, how they fit into it, and what they must do to thrive or survive (Alfred Adler, 1956). As they make these decisions, gain feedback, process the feedback and use it to refine their future decisions, an infant is literally developing neurological networks which serve as a type of "software," for responding to future circumstances. Through this process, a baby's interactions with their primary caregivers form the "blueprint" for all their future interactions. This is why babies are hardwired to connect with others, their brain structure is constantly developing according to the pattern of their interactions with people.

Let's look at how this happens. The attachment process unfolds as a response to a natural biological process called "homeostasis." Think of homeostasis as your body's way of achieving balance between states of alertness (or anxiety) and states of relaxation. This balance is necessary because, too much time in one or the other of these states is not good for a person's physical or emotional health. For example, when life is too stressful, we either shut down, or keep working in a state of partial panic or anxiety. No one can keep this up forever, which is why overly stressful work weeks are often followed by 48 hour Netflix binges. But if we have no stress or pressure to respond to, we either lose our motivation to do anything, or we start looking for something to stimulate us (eating out of boredom, arguing with people on Social Media, nagging our spouse or kids etc.).

These are examples of our body trying to strike *balance* between states of high-activity and states of relaxation. But during infancy, we are totally dependent on others to meet our needs and to help us maintain this balance. Without connection to others, infants cannot make this happen any more than they can keep themselves physically alive. This is why babies are wired to connect with us, but it's also why we're so irresistibly drawn to them. It is nature's way of making sure that the infant gets all the attention and care they need in order to survive and to develop.

Now, imagine you have a newborn infant. They probably sleep most of the day. If they're not hungry or wet, if nothing is poking them, if the temperature is fine, they're comfortable and quiet. But if they wake up and realize that their system is out of balance, they'll become uncomfortable, and dysregulated. How do they tell you about this? They use their only means of communication, they cry.

And what do we do when our infant cries? If we're nurturing caregivers, we go to them to figure out what's wrong. First, we check to see if the infant is wet or soiled. If they are, we put them somewhere stable and change their diaper. But what else are we doing while changing the diaper? We're probably looking at them, talking or cooing, smiling, etc. In doing so, we're meeting our infant's social and emotional need for connection, while meeting their physical need for a dry and comfortable diaper. Many of us talk to our baby about what we're doing and about the wet or soiled diaper and how much better they'll feel once they're dry. This may seem silly since we know the baby doesn't understand language yet. But we're helping them to self-regulate, physically and emotionally. Later, you'll see that this talking is playing a vital role in the infant's brain development and their ability to form attachments which will help them self-regulate later in life.

After tending to your infant, another hour or two goes by, during which the baby is calm and relaxed. Then the cycle begins anew. The baby has a need, lets us know by crying, and we respond. If it's been several hours, we'll probably check the diaper again. If it's dry, our next solution is likely to be feeding. Infants are most awake and aware while they're nursing. They're intently focused on their caregiver and on the world. Who hasn't held a baby while feeding and felt their intense, sustained gaze?

At seven to ten inches, the typical newborns' eyesight is twenty/twenty. This is the exact distance our eyes are from theirs during feeding! Babies need to be held in the closeness of our arms. And again, what are we doing while feeding? We are likely returning their gaze, stroking their head, talking, or singing. And if you think back to the last time you fed an infant, you probably remember them gripping your finger, touching your arm, or even putting their hand to your mouth. Skin-to-skin contact is an important factor in stimulating neurons and helping the brain develop its "software" for interacting with the world.

We guide our infant through this arousal-relaxation cycle many, many times each day—from need, to arousal, to satisfaction and eventually back to need again. And as we're guiding the infant through this process of self-regulation by meeting their physical, emotional and social needs, the infant's brain is processing stimuli and developing an understanding of how the process of self-regulation happens in the real world.

But what about when the infant is not wet, soiled, or hungry? There are times when you just don't know why they're crying. What do you do then? Again, attachment research tells you that the infant still has a need. Assuming nothing is poking them, or that they aren't sick, they probably just need to be *with* you. They want to be soothed and comforted. This is *not* manipulation (as Behaviorists Watson and Skinner presumed in the early part of the twentieth century). Infants are incapable of manipulation. They simply need what they need, and their need for connection is just as important as their need for a dry diaper. Remember the last time you were in this situation with an infant. What did you do, or say? Chances are you walked back and forth, you tried rocking them, you changed positions several times, all the while saying things like, "I know you're upset. I wish I knew what to do. I'm trying to figure out what you need," and you probably were doing some version of "Shshsh, shshsh." All of these are important for the infant's well-being. The infant is getting a sense of "feeling felt"—a thing which Dan Siegel describes as: the infant knowing that you are there, that you understand how they feel, and that you will continue to help them regulate.

A quick word here about stress. As you are doing all of the above, time passes. And what happens to *you* if you fail to soothe the infant? Your stress level is going up. You are becoming dysregulated. How well can you soothe an infant if *both* of you are in a dysregulated state? Slim to none. This is when most of us, if we have a good support system, will call on a partner, mother, or neighbor to help.

We progress through this "arousal-relaxation cycle" hundreds of times, during the first several months of an infant's life. As we do, the infant's needs are being met in a consistent and congruent way, through a meaningful connection with us. We are answering the infant's need for both physical and emotional care in loving, predictable and appropriate ways. As a result, the infant's brain structure is developing, and they begin to learn who they are, how the world operates and how the process of self-regulation happens. This is the process of secure attachment.

ON BRAIN STRUCTURE

In this section, we'll further clarify how secure attachment affects brain development by promoting causal thinking, trust, conscience development and the ability to delay gratification.

#1 Causal Thinking

One of the first things an infant learns is that the world is a *cause-and-effect system.* In other words, they learn that the world is predictable and consistent, and that there are rules which link actions to outcomes. But this only happens as a result of the "need, arousal, need met" cycle explained above. As the interactions with their caregiver occur, the infant learns, "When I have a need, I cry, and someone comes," or "When I don't feel right, I let people know, and my needs get met." Over time this translates to, "When A happens, B happens, and then C happens." This is called *causal thinking,* and it is primarily due to left-brain function. We use this function when in school. It determines our ability to read, to understand math and scientific concepts, and to eventually organize our time and understand consequences.

One of our most common behavior management strategies with young people is called *logical consequences,* and its dependent on the young person's capacity for causal thinking; that is, the skill of "If … then" thinking. Young people who have developed secure attachment will most likely have a solid grasp on this kind of thinking. Because of this, they'll do well in school, they'll respond to guidelines and structure, they'll learn to follow rules, and they'll develop flexible thinking (i.e., they'll be able to change their minds as required).

#2 TRUST

During the attachment process, the infant is also learning to trust. They're learning to trust that their primary caregiver(s) will be there when they need them. As stated earlier, interactions with primary caregivers form the basis for all our future relationships. At first, the infant builds his or her sense of trust with these caregivers. As a result, the infant will be able to trust others (family, friends, teachers, etc.) as he or she moves through childhood. This is Erikson's first stage of social-emotional development—trust vs. mistrust.

While the infant is learning to trust others, she's also learning to trust herself. She learns to trust that if she does not cry, her needs don't get met and her cycle remains dysregulated and unstable. She is learning, "I can control my world. I can make things happen. I can bring others to me." As her needs continue to get met in response to her cries—and later her words—she slowly develops self-efficacy, self-empowerment, and resilience.

#3 CONSCIENCE DEVELOPMENT

When we talk to babies, when we tell them what we are doing, when we use feeling words like "you are sad," or "you are uncomfortable," we are communicating that we understand their experience. We are helping them to "feel felt," a phrase coined by Dan Siegel in his book *Parenting From the Inside Out* (Siegel & Hartzell, 2014). This is how infants begin to understand emotions, and these emotions are the foundation through which they process their experiences in the world. Healthy people can understand and articulate their own emotions. Because of this, they can understand other people's emotions and experiences. This is the beginning of empathy and of moral judgment.

#4 ABILITY TO DELAY GRATIFICATION

Infants whose caregivers respond to their needs in a consistent and timely manner begin to understand that all their needs will eventually be met. As a result they will achieve the ability to wait patiently. Of course, most babies and toddlers aren't good at waiting. But if they've gotten off to the right start as an infant, they will learn in time. This ability to wait with confidence is a stunning indicator of the child's capacity to succeed later in life. For example, Walter Mischell's renowned "Marshmallow Test" required young children (four years old on average) to sit at a table with a marshmallow in front of them. They were told that as long as they waited a few minutes before eating it, they would get another one. Some children could wait, others couldn't. Remarkably, the experiment checked with those children later in life, finding that those who had waited were much more likely to succeed as adults. (Mischell, 2015).

So, to recap the four benefits of secure attachment:

1. Causal thinking.
2. Trust (of others and self)

3. Conscience development.
4. Ability to delay gratification.

As the above skills are developing, so is the child's intellectual potential (which is dependent on causal thinking) as well as their identity formation (which is founded on their ability to trust). Other secondary benefits include socialization and relationship skills, the ability to concentrate and handle stress, all as a result of these four foundational skills.

This happens because an infant with secure attachment has developed a solid brain structure. As they move into childhood and adolescence, they'll have self-efficacy skills, healthy self-esteem, and the ability to relate with others and to learn effectively. They will have good critical thinking and problem-solving skills. They will be confident and resilient and they'll have the ability to self-regulate in a healthy way. The best part is, we don't have to be perfect parents or caregivers to make this happen. We just have to be good enough and to be reasonably consistent.

But what's the outcome when secure attachment doesn't happen?

INSECURE ATTACHMENT

Infants born into unstable or unhealthy circumstances can't achieve secure attachment. Instead, they develop insecure attachment as a substitution to the real thing. There are several types of insecure attachment, but we'll cover three here.

#1 Insecure Ambivalent Attachment

Insecure ambivalent attachment happens when infants' needs are met inconsistently. For example, the caregiver may believe that picking up or holding the infant whenever she cries is "spoiling" her. So while the caregiver will consistently feed and change the diaper, they will only hold or cuddle them some of the time. This inconsistency leads to insecure ambivalent attachment. Another example might be when the infant has two different caregivers—one who answers all the baby's needs and another who might feed, change, and even hold her, but without any talking or eye contact. A third example might be a caregiver who can't always determine what the infant's need is. They change the diaper when the real need is for food. The result is that this child is confused. Sometimes all her needs are met, other times only some, and yet other times, the caregiver leaves her to cry.

Over time, the experience of this inconsistent care and nurturing will be "programmed" into the infant's brain structures. For this infant, the world may seem unpredictable, her belief unsure, and her feeling or emotional awareness will be incomplete, as will her eventual ability to wait or to self-regulate. As this infant moves into childhood and adolescence, it might be harder for her to learn cognitive skills (math, reading, and spelling). She might be unsure of herself and how others feel about her and she might have difficulty making or keeping friends, etc.

#2 *Avoidant Attachment*

Avoidant attachment happens when caregivers meet very, very few of the child's needs — physical or emotional. This is common in families where there is drug and/or alcohol use or abuse, or where caregivers have mental health problems. The caregivers either can't provide consistent, nurturing care or don't know how. As a result, the infant learns that his needs will rarely be met. He learns that others will not be there for him, that he cannot bring others to him, and/or no one understands his experience.

As this child moves through life, he will have little trust in himself or others. He will likely have a very hard time learning cognitive skills and following rules. He will find it hard to articulate his emotions or to sustain relationships. In extreme cases the infant will lose weight and become developmentally delayed. Many intensive care nurseries in hospitals care for these babies, and find that the babies have "failure to thrive syndrome." This is a sad condition where the baby experiences insufficient weight gain, inappropriate weight loss, or other physical insufficiencies.

#3 *Disorganized Attachment*

Disorganized attachment is a result of physical or emotional abuse to the infant or young child. It happens to infants and children who grow up with domestic violence or other chaos in their household. While there will be little or no opportunities for the child to form healthy attachments in these environments, the neurons in their brain still come pre-wired to connect and organize. These neural networks signal that the infant or child is hungry, tired, lonely or afraid etc. The child is literally wired to cry out for help. But if their primary caregivers perpetrate fear, discomfort, abuse, or chaos, the infant or child's basic needs for comfort and safety go unanswered. Since there is no way for the brain to process this lack of response, disorganization occurs. The infant's experience is so unstable, and yet so connected to their survival, they come to live with the constant subconscious fear that they will literally die.

Over time, this becomes what we consider chronic trauma. It manifests in childhood and adolescence in a variety of ways, but the most common is that the child becomes stuck in a survival state—or, what we call the "fight/flight/freeze" mode. This sabotages their ability to self-regulate. Without intervention, this child will have a very hard time learning in school, following rules, and relating to others in a healthy way. Subsequently, they will be at high risk for not developing a positive self-image. They will likely have negative self-esteem, a weak or nonexistent sense of self-efficacy low self-confidence and underdeveloped skills for self-regulation and self-control.

These are the three most common types of insecure attachment. Insecurely attached youth have great difficulty understanding and articulating their feelings and the feelings of others. They will seem to have no remorse over their behavior. Their response too most situations will be impulsive, and reactive, confrontational, rebellious or calloused. While they will still have developed their foundational brain structures, these structures will be compromised.

Attachment and the Brain

To summarize the impact of attachment on brain development, think of the difference between a carefully planned house built using good materials and a stable blueprint compared to one build using random scraps of garbage. This is comparable to the difference between brain structures developed through secure attachment and those developed through insecure attachment.

To put the impact of this difference into perspective, we'll use a brain model developed by Daniel Siegel and explained in his book *Parenting from the Inside Out*. Siegel asks us to consider the hand as a model for the brain. For example, hold up your hand and fold your thumb over your palm like the first hand position in figure 15.1. The part of your hand from the bottom of your palm and down into your wrist represents your brain stem. This is where your survival-based emotions and response are processed (i.e., fight, flight, freeze).

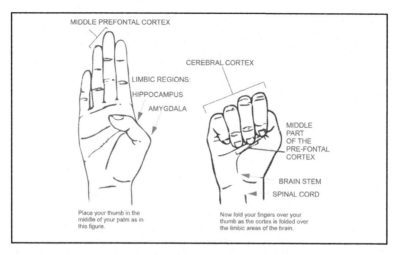

Place your thumb in the middle of your palm as in this figure.

Now fold your fingers over your thumb as the cortex is folded over the limbic areas of the brain.

Now, fold your fingers over your thumb as in the second hand position. Now your four fingers represent your brain's cortex. This is the part of the brain that regulates all your autonomic systems—breathing, heart rate, skin tone (via blood oxygenation), and sleep/wake cycles; it also keeps you safe.

The area of the cortex up front, where your fingernails are, is the *prefrontal cortex.* This is called the executive function brain—it is where thinking, planning, and processing information is stored. This is also the part of the brain that allows us to calm ourselves, make choices, and read body language. When we are really stressed or upset, or when we don't feel safe, the prefrontal cortex shuts down, and it no longer works in concert with the other parts of the brain.

To put this mental shift into perspective, straighten your fingers again so that your thumb is now exposed. This "exposure" of the brain stem represents what happens when you suddenly shift into flight, flight or freeze mode. Your higher-thinking mind "flips" off, leaving no "firewall" between the survival-based part of your brain and the real world. If you've ever been too angry or stressed to solve problems, make choices, or even control your emotions, you've experienced this mental state.

Youth who have secure attachment and good, solid foundational brain development have a brain structure in which all three parts of the brain (brain stem, limbic system, and executive function) are working together. They trust themselves and others. This means they can make choices and often perceive others accurately. When they do get upset or stressed, chances are they have some tools at their disposal that help them—they can talk to someone they trust, take some deep breaths, etc. Their ability to handle stress and to concentrate is likely pretty good.

For youth with insecure attachment—particularly those who have experienced chronic trauma in the form of abuse or neglect—the story is dramatically different. These youth frequently don't feel safe, don't feel they can trust others, may feel they have *not* been able to get their needs met, etc. And since their prefrontal cortex isn't wired to work in concert with the survival-based part of their brain, they will make rapid and unpredictable shifts between thinking with their higher faculties and thinking with their "animal brain."

These sudden shifts usually have nothing to do with the young person's present circumstances or with the caregivers, teachers, friends, they're interacting with. Instead, they have everything to do with the early messages (the blueprints) the young person formed in infancy about themselves, the world, and what they needed to do to survive. They are, in fact, often in the survival part of the brain, continually monitoring their safety, or in the emotional brain, wondering if they're loved. They're frequently in a heightened state of stress.

This heightened state of stress might not be outwardly noticeable. But research has shown that these youth have much faster heart rates and shallower breathing (the physical signs of heightened stress). Heightened stress drives these youth into fight-or-flight mode—also known as survival mode. What this means in the real world is that these young people tend to be very reactive—even small events or changes can set them off. They tend to be hypervigilant—constantly surveying their environment to ensure that they stay safe, and they often read other's emotions and actions inaccurately. For example, a child sitting next to them might get up to sharpen their pencil, accidentally knocking them with their elbow. The child with a history of chronic trauma may perceive this as an attack, flip into their survival brain out of fear, jump up, and hit the other child. What might look to the caregiver or teacher as unprovoked aggression is actually the child saving his own life. He hasn't made a conscious decision to do this. He is acting out of his survival instinct.

How Can We Help Youth with Histories of Chronic Trauma?

By now, you might be wondering if there's any hope for young people who have suffered insecure attachment. Of course, there are plenty of tools and strategies which can help young people with insecure attachment and/or histories of chronic trauma get a fresh start in life. But our focus should be on building the foundational brain structure and helping these young people learn self-regulation skills, so they can spend more time in the higher functioning part their brain.

We should not get tied up trying to answer the less significant questions like, "Why can't he read at grade level?" or "Why doesn't she have any friends?" or "Why doesn't he care when he hurts someone else?" These won't help us solve the problems caused by insecure attachment. The appropriate question is, "How do we help these youth build stronger, more resilient brains?"

You'll find 12 strategies in Part A of the *Positive Youth Guidance System* to help with this. You'll also find five strategies in Part B—which are specifically designed to develop the parts of the brain made deficient through insecure attachment. Take heart. The brain is incredibly flexible, even into the late years of our life. It can be retrained to "behave" in a way that's consistent with the benefits of secure attachment— and the *Positive Youth Guidance System* gives you the tools to make this happen.

362

REFERENCES

8 Health Benefits of a Healthy Self-Esteem. (2015, June 20). Retrieved March 27, 2018, from https://www.allegiancehealth. org/blog/women/8-health-benefits-healthy-Self-Esteem

Adler, A. (1956). *The individual psychology of Alfred Adler: A systematic representation in sections of his writings* (H.L. Ansbacher & R.R. Ansbacher Eds.). New York: Harper Perennial (original work published in 1956).

Adler, A. (2014). *Guiding the child: On the principles of individual psychology.* London: Routledge.

Akhtar, M. (2017, April 08). What is self-efficacy? Bandura's 4 Sources of Efficacy Beliefs. Retrieved March 27, 2018, from http://positivepsychology.org.uk/ self-efficacy-definition-bandura-meaning/

Bandura, A. (1977). *Social learning theory.* Englewood Cliffs: Prentice Hall.

Bandura, A. (2012). *Self-Efficacy: The exercise of control.* New York: W.H. Freeman.

Bandura, A., PhD. (2016, September 14). Social Learning Theory Bandura Social Learning Theory. Retrieved March 27, 2018, from https://www.learning-theories.com/social-learning-theory-bandura.html

Baumrind, D. (1967). Child care practices anteceding three patterns of preschool behavior. *Genetic Psychology Monographs,* 75(1), 43-88.

Becker-Weidman, A., & Shell, D. (2011). *Creating capacity for attachment: Dyadic developmental psychotherapy in the treatment of trauma-attachment disorders.* New York: Center for Family Development.

Bethell, C. D., Newacheck, P., Hawes, E., & Halfon, N. (2014). Adverse Childhood Experiences: Assessing the Impact On Health And School

Engagement And The Mitigating Role Of Resilience. *Health Affairs,* 33(12), 2106-2115. doi:10.1377/hlthaff.2014.0914

Branden, N. (1995). The Six Pillars of Self-Esteem, Kindle Edition. Retrieved March 27, 2018, from https://www.amazon.com.au/Six-Pillars-Self-Esteem-Nathaniel-Branden-ebook/dp/B007JK9BAY

Buri, J. R., Louis Elle, P. A., Misukanis, T. M., & Mueller, R. A. (1988). Effects of parental authoritarianism and authoritativeness on Self-Esteem. *Personality and Social Psychology Bulletin,* 14(2), 271-282.

Campbell, S., PhD. (2017, August 23). 8 Ways to Raise Kids to Have Exceptional Character. Retrieved March 15, 2018, from https://www.huffingtonpost.com/entry/8-ways-to-raise-kids-to-have-exceptional-character_us_599dc0eee4b02289f76191d0

Canaday, S. (2013, October 2). The High Price of self-awareness. Retrieved March 26, 2018, from https://www.psychologytoday.com/us/blog/you-according-them/201310/the-high-price-self-awareness.

Cherry, K. (2017, November 16). Find out Why Self-Esteem Is Important for Success. Retrieved March 27, 2018, from https://www.verywellmind.com/what-is-self-esteem-2795868

Cohen, A. R. (n.d.). Some implications of Self-Esteem for social influence. Retrieved March 27, 2018, from http://psycnet.apa.org/record/1960-07155-003

Coopersmith, S. (1967). *The Antecedents of Self-Esteem*. San Francisco, CA: W. H. Freeman & Company.

Coopersmith, S. (1990). *The antecedents of Self-Esteem*. Palo Alto, CA: Consulting Psychologists Press.

Croft, H., MD. (2016, March 25). How to Be a Good Communicator in a Relationship - Communicating - Relationships. Retrieved March 28, 2018, from https://www.healthyplace.com/relationships/communicating/how-to-be-a-good-communicator-in-a-relationship/

Dinkmeyer, D. C., & Dreikurs, R. (1965). *Encouraging children to learn: The encouragement process.* Englewood Cliffs, NJ: Prentice-Hall.

Does your Self-Esteem need a boost? (2017, July 12). Retrieved March 27, 2018, from https://www.mayoclinic. org/healthy-lifestyle/adult-health/in-depth/self-esteem/ art-20047976?pg=2

Dozier, M., & Lee, S. W. (1995). Discrepancies between self- and other-report of psychiatric symptomatology: Effects of dismissing attachment strategies. *Development and Psychopathology, 7*(01), 217. doi:10.1017/s095457940000643x

Dreikurs, R., & Cassel, P. (1991). *Discipline without tears / Featuring the Discipline Without Tears WorkBook, by David Kehoe.* New York: Plume.

Duckworth, A. (2017). *Grit: The power of passion and perseverance.* Place of publication not identified: Scribner.

Dweck, C. S. (2017). *Mindset: Changing the way you think to fulfil your potential.* New York: Robinson.

Enright, K. M., & Ruzicka, M. F. (1989). Relationship between perceived parental behaviors and the Self-Esteem of gifted children. *Psychology Report, 65*(3), 1st ser., 931-937.

Erikson's Psychosocial Theory of Human Development. (n.d.). Retrieved March 30, 2018, from https://

www.businessballs.com/self-management/
eriksons-psychosocial-theory-of-human-development-120/

Farmer, G. (Fall). 10 Benefits of self-awareness. Retrieved
March 26, 2018, from https://www.theselfawarenessguy.
com/64/10-benefits-of-self-awareness.

Felitti, V. J., Anda, R. F., Nordenberg, D., Williamson, D. F.,
Spitz, A. M.,

Edwards, V., Marks, J. S. (1998). Relationship of Childhood
Abuse and

Household Dysfunction to Many of the Leading Causes of
Death in Adults. *American Journal of Preventive Medicine,* 14(4),
245-258. doi:10.1016/s0749-3797(98)00017-8.

Healthy Lifestyle Adult Health, Mayo Clinic Retrieved March
19, 2019, from https://www.mayoclinic.org/healthy-lifestyle/
adult-health/in-depth/self-esteem/art-20047976

Fonvielle, D. (n.d.). What Are The Benefits Of
High Self Esteem? Retrieved March 27, 2018, from
http://www.alwaysgreater.com/achievements/
what-is-high-self-esteem-benefits-of-high-self-esteem.

Frank, M. A., PhD. (n.d.). Motivation: Intrinsic vs. Extrinsic by
Monica A.

Frank, Ph.D. Retrieved March 26, 2018, from https://www.
excelatlife.com/articles/intrinsic_motivation.htm

Frank, M. A., PhD. (2011). The Pillars of the Self-Concept: Self-Esteem and self-efficacy by Monica A. Frank, Ph.D. Retrieved March 27, 2018, from https://www.excelatlife.com/articles/self-esteem.htm

Furnham, A. (2011). *Managing People in a Downturn.* Basingstoke: Palgrave Macmillan.

Gamble, S. A., & Roberts, J. E. (2005). Adolescents' Perceptions of Primary Caregivers and Cognitive Style: The Roles of Attachment Security and Gender. *Cognitive Therapy and Research,* 29(2), 123-141. doi:10.1007/s10608-005-3160-7.

Gandhi, M. (n.d.). A quote by Mahatma Gandhi. Retrieved March 27, 2018, from https://www.goodreads.com/quotes/50584-your-beliefs-become-your-thoughts-your-thoughts-become-your-words.

Hazen, C., & Shaver, P. R. (1994). Attachment as an organizational framework for research on close relationships. *Psychological Inquiry,* 5, 1-22. Retrieved March 3, 2018.

Holmes, J. (2014). *John Bowlby and attachment theory.* London: Routledge, Taylor & Francis Group.

Howard, K., Martin, A., Berlin, L. J., & Brooks-Gunn, J. (2011, January). Early Mother-Child Separation, Parenting, and Child Well-Being in Early Head Start Families. Retrieved March 30, 2018, from https://www.ncbi.nlm.nih.gov/pmc/articles/PMC3115616/

Jordan, A. (n.d.). John Dewey on Education: Impact & Theory. Retrieved March 27, 2018, from https://study.com/academy/lesson/john-dewey-on-education-impact-theory.html.

Kaslow, N. J., Adamson, L. B., & Collins, M. H. (2000). A Developmental Psychopathology Perspective on the Cognitive Components of Child and Adolescent Depression. *Handbook of Developmental Psychopathology,* 491-510. doi:10.1007/978-1-4615-4163-9_26

Klebanov, M. S., & Travis, A. D. (2015). *Felliti in The critical role of parenting in human development.* New York, NY: Routledge, Taylor & Francis Group.

Kuiper, N. A., Olinger, L. J., & Swallow, S. R. (1987). Dysfunctional attitudes, mild depression, views of self, self-consciousness, and social perceptions. *Motivation and Emotion,* 11(4), 379-401. doi:10.1007/bf00992851

Leary, M. R., & Baumeister, R. F. (2004, November 18). The nature and function of Self-Esteem: Sociometer theory. Retrieved March 27, 2018, from https://www.sciencedirect.com/science/article/pii/S0065260100800039

Lewis, M. (1990). *Self-knowledge and social development in early life. In L. A. Pervin (Ed.), Handbook of personality* (pp. 277-300). New York: Guilford Press.

Lewis, M., & Brooks-Gunn, J. (1979). Social Cognition and the Acquisition of Self. doi:10.1007/978-1-4684-3566-5

Lowry, L. (n.d.). What Is Behaviour Regulation? And What Does It Have To Do With Language Development? Retrieved March 28, 2018, from http://www.hanen.org/helpful-info/articles/what-is-behaviour-regulation--and-what-does-it-hav.aspx

Maccoby, E. E., & Martin, J. A. (1983). *Socialization in the context of the family: Parent-child interaction. In E. M. Hetherington (Ed.), Handbook of child psychology: Vol. 4. Socialization, personality, and social development* (4th ed., pp. 1 – 101). New York : Wiley.

Main, M., & Solomon, J. (n.d.). *Discovery of an insecure-disorganized/disoriented attachment pattern. In T. B. Brazelton & M. W. Yogman (Eds.), Affective development in infancy* (pp. 95-124). Westport, CT, US: Ablex Publishing (pp. 95-124). Westport, CT, US: Ablex Publishing.

McLeod, S. (2012, January 01). Saul McLeod. Retrieved March 27, 2018, from https://www.simplypsychology.org/self-esteem.html

Meyer, I. H. (2003). Prejudice, social stress, and mental health in lesbian, gay, and bisexual populations: Conceptual issues and research evidence. *Psychological Bulletin,* 129(5), 674-697. doi:10.1037/0033-2909.129.5.674

Miller, D. F. (2016). *Positive child guidance.* Boston, MA, USA: Cengage Learning.

Mischel, W. (2015). *The marshmallow test: Why self-control is the engine of success.* New York: Little, Brown and Company.

370

Montemayor, R., & Eisen, M. (1977). The development of self-conceptions from childhood to adolescence. *Developmental Psychology*, 13(4), 314-319. doi:10.1037//0012-1649.13.4.314

Morin, A. (2006). Levels of consciousness and self-awareness: A comparison and integration of various neurocognitive views. *Consciousness and Cognition*, 15(2), 358-371. doi:10.1016/j. concog.2005.09.006

Morvitz, E., & Motta, R. W. (1992). Predictors of Self-Esteem: The roles of parent-child perceptions, achievement, and class placement. *Journal of Learning Disabilities*, 25(1), 72-80.

Nelsen, J., Lott, L., & Glenn, H. S. (2007). *Positive discipline A-Z: 1001 solutions to everyday parenting problems*. New York: Three Rivers.

Nelson, J. (2018, March 24). About Positive Discipline. Retrieved March 28, 2018, from https://www.positivediscipline. com/about-positive-discipline

Positive Self Image and Self Esteem. (n.d.). Retrieved March 27, 2018, from http://www.mtstcil.org/skills/image-1.html

Roberts, D. F., Henriksen, L., & Foehr, U. (n.d.). *Adolescents and the media*.

In: Lerner R, Steinberg L, editors. Handbook of Adolescent Psychology. (2nd ed., 204b). Hoboken, NJ: John Wiley and Sons.

Self-concept. (n.d.). Retrieved March 26, 2018, from https://www.merriam-webster.com/dictionary/self-concept

Self-image. (n.d.). Retrieved March 26, 2018, from https://www.merriam-webster.com/dictionary/self-image

Self-perception theory. (2018, March 21). Retrieved March 26, 2018, from https://en.wikipedia.org/wiki/Self-perception_theory

Shanker, S., & Barker, T. (2017). *Self-reg: How to help your child (and you) break the stress cycle and successfully engage with life.* NY, NY: Penguin Books.

Siegel, D. J., & Hartzell, M. (2014). *Parenting from the inside out: How a deeper self-understanding can help you raise children who thrive.* Brunswick, Vic.: Scribe Publications.

Stein, H. T. (n.d.). Adlerian Child Guidance Principles. Retrieved March 28, 2018, from http://www.adlerian.us/guid.htm

Stosny, S., PhD. (2011, October). self-regulation To feel better, focus on what is most important. *Psychology Today.*

The Merriam-Webster Collegiate dictionary. (2016). Springfield, MA: Merriam-Webster.

The World's Most Trusted Dictionary Provider. (n.d.). Retrieved March 27, 2018, from https://www.oxforddictionaries.com/

Tjan, A. K. (2015, February 11). 5 Ways to Become More Self-Aware. Retrieved March 26, 2018, from https://hbr.org/2015/02/5-ways-to-become-more-self-aware

Vago, D. R., & Silbersweig, D. A. (2012). Self-awareness, self-regulation, and self-transcendence (S-ART): A framework for understanding the neurobiological mechanisms of mindfulness. *Frontiers in Human Neuroscience*, 6. doi:10.3389/fnhum.2012.00296

Vago, D. R., & Silbersweig, D. A. (2012). Self-awareness, self-regulation, and self-transcendence (S-ART): A framework for understanding the neurobiological mechanisms of mindfulness. *Frontiers in Human Neuroscience*, 6. doi:10.3389/fnhum.2012.00296

Washbrook, E., Waldfogel, J., & Moullin, S. (2017, July 26). 40% OF CHILDREN MISS OUT ON THE PARENTING NEEDED TO SUCCEED IN LIFE. Retrieved March 28, 2018, from https://www.suttontrust.com/newsarchive/40-children-miss-parenting-needed-succeed-life-sutton-trust/

Weissman, P., & Hendrick, J. (2014). *The whole child: Developmental education for the early years*. Boston: Pearson.

Williams, S. (n.d.). Self-awareness and Personal Development. Retrieved March 26, 2018, from http://www.wright.edu/~scott.williams/LeaderLetter/selfawareness.htm#How_Self-Awareness_Makes_You_More

Wood, J. K., & Fabrigar, L. R. (2015, November 30). Attitudes. Retrieved March 27, 2018, from http://www.oxfordbibliographies.com/view/document/obo-9780199828340/obo-9780199828340-0074.xml

Zeigler-Hill, V. (2013). *Self-Esteem*. New York, NY: Psychology Press.

Zimmerman, B. J. (2002). Becoming a Self-Regulated Learner: An Overview. *Theory Into Practice*, 41(2), 64-70.

AUTHOR BIOGRAPHY

Dr. Kim Metcalfe has dedicated the last 15 years of her life training over 8,000 college aged students in best principles and strategies for helping youth reach their full cognitive, creative, emotional, social, and physical potential. Dr. Kim's work centers around the importance of mental and emotional well-being. "The best way to create appropriate learning environments is to nurture the emotional, social, and creative needs of every person within it." This is the basis of the "connection" component of equity, trauma informed care and anti-bully practices. As a consultant, trainer, and youth and school advocate, Dr. Kim is passionate about facilitating practices that transform institutions into communities that support teaching and learning.

Dr. Kim developed the Positive Youth Guidance System to train adults in strategies for making "meaningful connections" with youth and The Identity Platform to get teens re-excited about life outside of the digital world.

Dr. Kim is a member of the Positive Discipline Association; a Certified Positive Discipline Trainer for K-12 classrooms, parents, and early childhood education settings. She is faculty of the CEO Space Youth Program; the founder and executive director of two organizations, Abbey's Purple Winged Angels Foundation and Dr. Kim's XtraOrdinary Youth. Both of these organizations envision a world that intentionally moves youth into productive, meaningful, joyful, and ethical lives.

Made in the USA
Monee, IL
26 November 2019

17537644R00223